The Best I Can Do

A Panoply of Humorous Essays and Light Verse

John Branning

By the same author

Selfie-Facing: Analog Musings in a Digital World
Rhymes of Moral Turpitude: The Trump Poems: Year One
Rhymes of Moral Turpitude: The Trump Poems: Year Two
Rhymes of Moral Turpitude: The Trump Poems: Special Impeachment Edition
Keys to the Truculent Me: And Other Things That Drive Me Crazy

The Best I Can Do

Copyright © 2012-2022 by John Branning

All rights reserved.

John Branning
Winthrop ME 04364

This book or any portion thereof may not be reproduced or used in any manner whatsoever without the express written permission of the publisher except for the use of brief quotations in a book review or scholarly journal.

Some of these materials first appeared in the publications listed above.

First Printing: September 2022
Pusillanimous Books

www.JohnBranning.com

ISBN: 978-0-9970773-9-1

To my wife and son and the various cats who have owned us over the years.

"Laughter is the sun that drives winter from the human face." - Victor Hugo

If that's true, then please apply sunscreen before reading any further.

Contents

Foreword 7
In the Beginning There Were Some (Not-So-Good) Words 9
    To Sleep; Perchance To Snore 9
Languish and Other Near-Homonyms 13
    Language-ing by the Pool 13
    Written Too Hard 15
    Apostrophe for Services Rendered 20
    A Bad Case of Subjunctivitis 21
A Prize Idiot 23
    Blue Genius 23
    My Reign in MacArthur Grant Park 25
    Pooh-Pooh Pulitzers 27
    Brain on my Parade 28
Dissemblance of Things Past 31
    Holy Molar 31
    Making a Bee Line 34
    Racked with Gelt 37
    Recipe for Disaster 40
    Let's Face It 44
    Climb Every Mantra 47
    Here's Everything I Know About Wine in Five Minutes or (Much) Less 50
    Live Forever or Diet in the Attempt 52
    Jest the Facts 53

List Less 55
- Aphorism Schism 55
- Bitter Patter 56
- Adage Before Beauty 58
- Goal all the Way 59
- My Search for Happiness (on Google) 63
- Songs of Romance and Passion, Updated 66
- Not If I CPU First 67
- Philosophers Stoned 68
- Making a Demi-Glace of Myself 74
- Senior Winces 76

Rhymes A-Wastin' (Part I) 81
- What If – 81
- Sorry Seems to be the Hardest Word 82
- Pardon Me? 83
- Big Man on Hippocampus 84
- Bul-let Us Pray 86
- War Zeroes 87
- No Guts, No Glory 89
- Sob Stories 91
- On a Scale of One to Contentious 92
- Me-Day 93
- Prodding the Squad 95
- Wretched Refusal 96
- Shooting My Mouth Off 97
- Elements of a Perfect Phone Call 98
- Id Pro Quo 99

Don't You Know It 100

Kiss My Aspirations Goodbye 101

I Am the Very Muddle 102

Son of a Bleach 104

Better to Remain Silent 105

Stop Picking on Me 107

Brain He Lacks 107

Scrambled Egghead 108

He's Mailing It In Now 109

Deduction Reasoning 110

Relapse in Judgment 112

Transitioning Bender 113

Distressed Address 114

A Riotous Success 115

Vlad All Over 116

Bunker Mentality 117

Overdue Rant 118

Unbottled Rage 119

Marital Blitz 121

Speaker of the House 121

Death Fakes a Holiday 123

Really in the Ears (with apologies to Steely Dan) 126

My Bathroom Innovation Will Make You Flush
with Excitement 128

The Princess and the Pee Stain 131

Drain the Swamp 133

Dogged by a Pet Name 135

Teller I Love Her 136

Brow Beaten 139

New Skin off my Nose 141

Stairing Contest 143

Rhymes A-Wastin' (Part II) 147

Cereal Killer 147

Tüber 148

Repast Due 148

Birder Most Fowl 149

Spritz Impossible 150

Hexed Libris 150

Schmooze Operator 151

Grand Canal Seizure 152

Crash Decision 153

House of Buggin' 153

Special Saucer 154

Marching Madness 155

Getting Over the Humpback 156

Let's Be Frankfurter 156

Here's the Scoop 157

Running Short 158

Presents Aren't Accounted For 159

River-Horsing Around 160

Hook, Line and Blinker 160

Casting a Spell 161

Creepy Sleepytime 162

Spread Alert 162

    Come and Flamingo 163

    A-Peel-ing Behavior 164

Just For Pun 165

    Don't Ass, Don't Yell 165

    Blow Me 167

    The Right to Bare Arms 169

    Bitcoin, Broketooth 170

    Smoke Scream 173

    Speaker of the Hows 175

    Holland Tunnel Vision 177

    Whatever You Do, Don't Faucet 179

    Macramé-be Not 182

Afterward 185

About the Author 187

Foreword

Thank you for your purchase of this book. Or, if you are just thumbing through a copy while killing time somewhere, I trust you washed your hands before doing so.

This collection contains pieces covering a ten-year span. I started a humor blog, called *FactsOptional*, in December 2012 and have continued posting right up until (and, I anticipate, beyond) the moment you are reading this sentence.

Along the way, in addition to the humor (or, at least, attempts at) posted on that blog, I also branched into political commentary via light verse, which eventually resided at a site called *The Trump Poems*. I also continued in the verse vein with comments on news-adjacent oddities (non-political, although these days it seems everything is political) under the banner *Rhyme for the News*.

In 2022, I consolidated all of these blogs into one easy-to-overlook website, *JohnBranning.com*. That's where all previous posts have been archived and where anything new that comes to mind is affixed.

All of which leads to this compilation of jocular reflection and commentary – some of which were previously-published, others are newly-published, and a few should never-have-been-published.

I admire the writing of so many humorists, essayists, columnists, poets, novelists… far too many to list here. I trust their influences upon me are opaque and not too blatant. To paraphrase a quote, some version of which has been attributed to any number of creative luminaries: *"Immature artists copy; great artists steal."*

Me? I type.

John Branning / Winthrop, Maine / August 2022

In the Beginning There Were Some (Not-So-Good) Words

The very first entry I posted on the FactsOptional blog, in December 2012, was entitled, "Make Your Resume Stand Out." Having recently re-read it for consideration in this collection – it's clear that piece did *not* stand out... In fact, none of the four pieces from that first blogging month are worthy of revisiting.

Here's the first thing after starting this adventure that I feel has any merit:

To Sleep; Perchance To Snore
(January 22, 2013)

My wife Carol began snoring sometime during her pregnancy with our son Josh, so that means it was almost thirty years ago that our sleep patterns were first disturbed. When I say "our sleep patterns," I mean "my sleep pattern." She tends to sleep through the commotion. My favorite comment is when she denies she's been snoring because, "I'm not even asleep yet." Well, if there's such a thing as waking dreams, then I guess there can be waking snoring.

At first, I'd gently and affectionately rub her back to interrupt the noise and lull her back into a quieter rest. Over the years, the volume, intensity, and duration became increasingly cacophonous, so that gentle touch became a more muscular, less empathy-driven approach. I'd shake her shoulder, and if that didn't work, sometimes I'd put my hand on her back and push. Rarely, however, were any of these efforts successful in the long term (defined as "at least two hours of relative quiet"). As her snoring became more persistent, and my efforts to quell it provided a decreasing return on investment, I finally moved out of our bed together and started to sleep in the guest room, eliminating the disturbance for both of us. This caused some feelings of abandonment, so every now and then I'd spend the night back in the queen-size to reinstate the cuddling, spooning, and general sense of togetherness that sleeping separately undermined. Rarely, however, would we make it through an entire night in the same bed. At some point, when one of my REM cycles was near an end, her snoring would slice through the thin membrane of near-consciousness and wake me up. I'd lie there, frustrated and pounding the pillow, and finally move down the hall back into my own sleep sanctum.

I tried earplugs but found them uncomfortable – I'd fall asleep, but wake up after ninety minutes or so feeling as though balloons were in my ears, about to pop. I found if I went to bed first it sometimes gave me a chance to fall asleep before Carol climbed into bed, and occasionally I'd make it through a good portion of the night not hearing her – but only one out of every five or six evenings. We tried various "white noise" strategies with no greater success. At one point, my wife asked her doctor if anything could be done to treat her snoring. After an examination, he said there were two courses of treatment – either surgery to remove her uvula or examination in a sleep clinic since she exhibited the classic symptoms of sleep apnea. She dismissed the idea of surgery (I agreed) and instead spent a night in the sleep clinic under observation (during which I slept soundly). A few days later, she picked up a CPAP machine, a device designed to keep her airway open while sleeping and thereby eliminate the snoring. However, the machine made quite a racket of its own, and the mask she had to wear left her skin grooved and irritated in the morning. The CPAP went to the back of our closet, and the snoring resumed.

Several years ago, I accepted a job offer that would move us to Boston. I came up first, staying in a studio apartment on my own until Carol was ready to leave her job and make the transition. Ironically, in my Boston apartment I finally got comfortable sleeping with earplugs, since my studio was next to the Mass Pike and across from the Back Bay train station. Between relentless traffic noise and early morning train arrivals, earplugs were required if I were to sleep at all. After several months we were finally reunited in our new city and a larger (and quieter) loft apartment in the South End. Now that I was earpluggable, we resumed sleeping in the same bed with greater success. There were still some nights when I was restless, or Carol's snoring was so extreme that I would move to a small bed tucked beneath the loft stairs, but usually we were able to make it through the night together. Our son, then age twenty, chose to stay behind when Carol moved north, but six months later decided to come to Boston to be closer to us and so stayed "temporarily" in our loft. It turned out to be a six-month residency. Josh slept in that little bed under the stairs, so I was forced to remain in the loft regardless of my restlessness or that night's decibel level. Now that my option to relocate was eliminated, it seemed Carol's snoring intensified. I'm sure that was just my perception, but still… even the earplugs didn't help.

Our son has since moved into his own apartment, and we've moved from the loft to a much larger two-bedroom space in Cambridge. Except when we have overnight company visiting, the guest room is "my room." Our relationship is still a little unsettled by not always sleeping together after so many years as a happy and loving couple, but we've come to the realization that we get along better during our waking hours together when we're both well-rested from the night before.

In those first months in Boston, shortly after Josh came to stay with us, Carol went out of town for a few days to attend a conference. I had the loft bedroom all to myself and looked forward to a few nights' worth of deep, quiet sleep. I woke up after a very satisfactory slumber the first morning after she'd left and went downstairs to get ready for work. My son began to rouse after I came down. I asked him how he'd slept and he mumbled, "Not very well." When I asked him why not, he raised himself on one elbow, glared at me from beneath heavy eyelids, and said, "Because you SNORED ALL NIGHT."

Languish and Other Near-Homonyms

I sometimes writes about grammar and how it ~~flummoxen~~ flummoxes me.

Language-ing by the Pool
(February 6, 2013)

I've been speaking English my entire life (minus the first 18 months or so), and reading and writing it nearly as long — and somehow only recently have I become aware of the "Oxford comma." I mean, I knew what it was, but I just didn't realize it was a part of punctuation that had this particular name attached to it, like "capital letters" and "missed my period." (And before we go any further here — was the period in that last sentence supposed to be placed within or outside of the quotation marks? Just to be clear, I'm not talking about the "missed" period.)

Now it seems not a week goes by that some twit… er, I mean some tweet, or a blog post or some other forum for lexicographic commentary references the Oxford comma. I'd heard of Oxford collars, and Oxford shoes, and the Oxford Press (where, I presume, one would have a shirt with an Oxford collar ironed). I do recall learning not to place a comma before the last item in a series. Said comma, when placed, is known as the Oxford comma. Are there names for other kinds of commas? The only other one I know by name is a "medically-induced comma," which is what language-obsessives are placed into after their participation in frenzied debates regarding the disregard of proper grammatical practices causes them to stroke out.

I won't rehash the two sides to the Oxford comma issue here since there are many other and more-learned references one could Google if one were so inclined. Or more than one of you, if you can persuade your friend to join you in Googling. However, this kerfuffle has caused me to investigate what other rules of grammar, spelling and writing (or should that be "grammar, spelling, and writing"? or "grammar, spelling, and writing?")... what was I saying? Oh yes — here are some other grammatical rules with which I've recently become reacquainted with:

- "i" before "e," except after 3:00 PM.
- Don't leave a participle dangling; make a clean break from the relationship and then walk away.
- The plural of any singular noun ending in "y" is more than you'll ever need.
- "Who" and "Whom" are frequently confused for one another, but not as often now that "Whom" got its hair cut.
- "Lay" is an intransitive verb; "lie" is what I just told you.
- Proper use of "its" vs. "it's" can be easily resolved by reading your sentence out loud and substituting "it is" for whichever word you used. If the sentence sounds silly, try reading it again in your normal voice.
- Should it be "between you and I" or "between you and me"? Sorry, honey — I broke it off with you months ago; get over it. And take your participle with you.
- Context is often helpful when trying to determine which word is correct. For example, telling your sister-in-law, "You've put on a *complement* of 20 pounds since I last saw you" would not be taken as a *compliment*.
- If you can count it, use "fewer." If you can't count it, then a spreadsheet is required.
- Some common phrases just confound all logic. As an example, you'll ask for "a pair of scissors" when you only want one scissor. The plural of "moose" is also "moose," which is why they so rarely come when called — they're not sure which one of them you're talking to.
- A semi-colon is what many people are forced to use after a bowel resection.
- Did you know you should place a predicate pronoun after an infinitive? Me neither.

- "Hopefully" is a dangling modifier. Fortunately, the attendant will point it out before you leave the men's room.

Those of we whom are interested in the dynamics of the English language are familiar with *The Elements of Style*, which is often referred to as "Strunk and White" after it is two co-authors, some guy named Strunk and the editor E. B. White. Many years ago, I had the pleasure of speaking with the late Mr. White (in this context, late means "deceased" as opposed to "not on time." However, I am fairly certain I spoke with him before he ceased being.). I'll never forget what he said to me: "How did you get my phone number? Stop bothering me, for crisssakes. Your giving me a heart attack." I didn't have the strunk to tell him he'd mis-spoken; surely he meant to say, "Your giving I a heart attack."

Hopefully, upon all of you a similar impression I has made.

Written Too Hard
(September 11, 2017)

It seems at some point every author puts down in writing their process for... putting things down in writing. Sometimes they even write an entire book about... how to write a book.

Typically, these are authors of some renown (think Anne Lamott, Stephen King, Ray Bradbury, Annie Dillard, many others). However, I think it's easy — from their vantage point of having already achieved some level of critical success (which I realize is an arbitrary measure, but William Shatner has something like thirty books to his credit and no one is clamoring to learn about *his* process) to look back and say, "This is how I did it." What early-in-their-careers writers really need is someone to tell them in real-time, "This is how I'm doing it."

Pine no more. From the vantage point of someone still lusting after that first, big, ~~lucrative~~ critically-acclaimed score, here are my thoughts on the ~~grift~~ craft of writing:

Think of things. I sit, sometimes with a glass of water, perhaps a cup of coffee, occasionally a Scotch or Dr. Pepper and vodka, and open up my mind to thoughts: "What happened to me today?" "What happened to me yesterday?" "What would happen to me tomorrow if I woke up and found I was the Count of Monte Cristo?" "What am I making for dinner tonight?" "Uh oh, did I forget to tell my wife about the notice from the IRS we got in the mail?" "What if Donald Trump was in an accident and awoke to find his head grafted onto Barack Obama's body, à la *The Thing With Two Heads*?" Now I'm on to something… I bet Trump's sweaters are already large enough that Obama could just slip in there next to him without stretching the necks any further.

Write them down. This may seem obvious, but how many times have you heard someone say, "I'm carrying around this great idea for a novel in my head," or, "One of these days I'm going to write a book about my experiences in the waste removal industry." This next point is very important: *You can not call yourself a writer if you haven't actually written anything down.* Until you do, you can call yourself an intellectual, or a spoken-word artist, or William Shatner — but not a "writer."

- There are those who still write out their entire book in longhand, on legal pads, or in Composition notebooks. Others use index cards or sticky notes to outline the plot and capture key character traits, affixing them to the wall in order to map out the flow of the novel-in-progress. Some still bang 'em out on a typewriter. Many of us make use of modern technology and write on a computer or tablet. The great advantage here is that there are a variety of software programs to check spelling, grammar. And punctuation; Best of all, if you've got internet access it's a piece of cake to copy and paste something like

Machiavelli's *The Prince*, revise it just enough to avoid charges of plagiarism, and then publish it under the title *The Art of the Deal*.

Begin with the end in mind. I guess I should have started with this... Sure, you've got a great idea for a book ("Two good-looking people have lots of kinky sex.") — but where are you going with that? What will happen at the <u>end</u> of the story? They get tired and fall asleep? He puts his clothes on and goes back home to his wife? They have sex again? They fall in love, get married, have kids, move to the suburbs and she is beyond miserable every goddam day? You've got to figure out a satisfactory ending, otherwise you'll just write and write and write and end up like George R. R. Martin, frantically cranking out his *Game of Thrones* fantasy books in order to keep up with the wildly popular HBO adaptation of them, leaving himself barely any time to count his hundreds of millions of dollars. Hmm... I'm no longer seeing the downside here.

Write every day. If you're really serious about writing — I mean *really serious*; you've bought a new pen and everything — then writing is something you've got to commit to. (Or, as my grammar program is begging me to say: "... something to which you've got to commit.") Writing is an exercise program for your mind, and just as you don't get any benefits from no longer hopping on that $1500 treadmill you insisted you needed to get into shape and instead are now using to dry your sweaters, you need to exercise your writing muscle on a consistent, even unrelenting, basis, even whe

- [NOTE TO SELF: Will come back to finish this point after *Judge Judy*.]

Include a variety of sentence types. Most grammatical guides will claim there are four types of sentences:

1. <u>Simple sentences</u> contain just one independent clause: "Santa loaded the sleigh."
2. <u>Compound sentences</u> contain two independent clauses: "Santa loaded the sleigh, and his wife baked cookies."
3. <u>Complex sentences</u> contain both an independent and dependent clause: "After Santa left to deliver presents, his wife staged an orgy with the elves."
4. <u>Compound-complex sentences</u> contain at least two independent and one dependent clause: "After Santa left to deliver presents, his wife staged an orgy with the elves, and then Santa came home to a kitchen empty other than for a plate of freshly-baked cookies."

Including all of these sentence types in your writing will really increase your word count, and the paragraphs will practically write themselves. However, there is yet another type of sentence to consider: the <u>suspended sentence</u>. You use this when you want to generate suspense in your narrative:

- "Santa suspected his wife was cuckolding him during his yearly absences, so with a freshly-baked cookie in one hand and a .357 Magnum in the other, he snuck back into the workshop before anyone realized he had returned from his trip around the world."

Use lots of adjectives. Those ~~venomous~~ ~~venereal~~ venerable guides to the art of stylish writing, Strunk and White, command us to "[O]mit needless words." I disagree. Which of the following statements do you feel makes its meaning clearer?

- "Get over here."
- "Get your goddam ass over here NOW!"

18

I certainly had a clearer understanding of my father's meaning when he beckoned me using the wordier version of that statement.

To prove my point, here's a quote directly from Strunk and White: "*The fact that* is an especially debilitating expression." Why do they say "especially debilitating?" The fact that they included a superfluous adjective suggests that even those ~~degenerate~~ venerated champions of clarity in word choice sometimes felt the need to be very emphatic.

(Strunk also objected to the use of *very*, calling it and other similar modifiers — *rather, little, pretty* — "leeches that infest the pond of prose." But believe me — I would be very hesitant to go swimming in a pond filled with leeches. *Especially* prose-infested leeches.)

Be open to criticism. After publishing my first book, I received a number of laudatory, 5-star reviews on Amazon — along with a 1-star review from someone who expressed his profound disappointment with it. Instead of being crushed, I carefully considered his online response, reflected upon what I could have done differently, and then tracked his IP address in order to find his physical location so I could leave a flaming sack of dog shit on his front porch. Without his candid assessment of my work, I never would have found the courage to express my thoughts in that way.

Compare my insights above against what other "successful" writers have said about the process:

- Jack Kerouac: "It ain't whatcha write, it's the way atcha write it."
    - I believe Kerouac's amphetamine habit led to the term "speed typist."
- Margaret Atwood: "A word after a word after a word is power."
    - But not just any any any word.

- Maya Angelou: "There is no greater agony than bearing an untold story within you."
    - I guess she never passed a kidney stone.

Upon reflection, maybe there are some advantages to my remaining very obscure. Especially after offering you this debilitating insight into my process.

Apostrophe for Services Rendered
(October 14, 2017)

Hello, I'm an apostrophe
and I reside up top, you see.
I indicate possessiveness,
yet people won't give me a rest.
I also let you take two words
and shorten them to sound absurd.
I often find that I'm misplaced;
misused; abused; on signs defaced.
I'm wrongly used to make one plural —
you shouldn't call two sisters "girl's."
And to this day I have not got
a clue how "won't" comes from "will not."
Sometimes I see a superscript
linked to a footnote, tightly clipped.
But otherwise, I feel alone
residing up here, on my own.
Some write: "A dog licks it's behind,"
as if that placement I won't mind.
You can't distinguish "its" from "it's?"
Then your a bunch of stupid shit's.

A Bad Case of Subjunctivitis
(July 24, 2018)

Today we will investigate one of the dark caverns of the grammatical underworld — **diacritical marks**.

First of all, let's define the word *diacritical*. This is what happens when your mother, on her deathbed, uses her last breath to tell you what a disappointment you've been to her your entire life.

Another word for a diacritical mark is a *glyph*. A glyph is an unpronounceable word, since it contains no vowels. Vowels are the letters *a, e, i, oh no, yoo-hoo* and, sometimes, *y*. This, however, is not one of those times.

There are few words native to the English language requiring diacriticals. Most of the words that do and are now part of our everyday speech have been imported from other countries, often without a tariff assessed and therefore leading to the current trade war. Perhaps the best-known example to illustrate this is *piña colada*, with the little wiggly bugger over the "n" called a *tilde* (which is pronounced "TILL-day," as in, "I'm going to drink piña coladas all through the night and *tilde*-light comes.").

Another diacritical is the *umlaut*, which has its origins in Germanic languages. (Have you ever noticed how animated German people are when speaking? That's because theirs is a -manic language.) In English, however, it is often confused with its identical twin, the *diaeresis*. The diaeresis is found only when discussing the Brontë sisters (which no one ever does), or when reading articles in *The New Yorker* magazine. *The New Yorker* (yes, *The New Yorker*) is also notorious for doubling down on a consonant before a suffix, such as in "focussed" and "traveller." I, personally, double down only when I'm holding an ace and the dealer draws a bust card. Anyway — during a recent vacation, I suffered from a bout of traveller's diaeresis, but a few swigs of Maälox took care of it.

And then there are the accents: *acute* and *grave*. An *acute* accent is like the one the character Fez used in the sitcom *That 70's Show*. A *grave* accent is adoptted by Meryl Streep in every movie for which she wins Best Actress.

Finally, let's review use of the *cedilla*, which is a hook or tail affixed underneath certain letters. *Soupçon* is a good example here: when I was a youngster, my mother would call out "*Soupçon!*" when lunch was ready. By the time I reached the table, everyone else would already have a heaping serving and all that remained for me were a few brothy spoonfuls, containing neither chicken nor stars. I would burst into tears and my mother would console me by saying, "You are destined to be a disappointment to me your entire life."

Well, at the risk of disappointing *you*, dear reader – I'll bring this to a close. Keep your eyes open for our next topic of discussion: *Editing While Intoxicated, or 80-Proofreading*.

A Prize Idiot

On multiple occasions I've expressed my pique at not receiving the kind of international acclaim and peer recognition that only I believe my work deserves. The next few posts all touch on that misplaced sense of snubbery.

Blue Genius
(September 29, 2015)

Well, they've just announced the 2015 MacArthur Fellows — i.e., the "genius grants" — and again my name is nowhere to be found on the list. I checked, twice. Honestly, I'm not sure how much longer I can sustain this level of brilliance without the appropriate recognition. Inspiration is fleeting.

This year's honorees each receive a stipend of $625,000, payable in quarterly installments over five years. While I'm not quite sure what a "stipend" is, my disappointment isn't all about the money. Yes, it's largely about the money but there's also the component of being acknowledged for what I've done creatively and what I could do in the future with $625K burning a hole in my pocket. The foundation website mentions the award permits recipients "the flexibility to pursue their own artistic, intellectual, and professional activities in the absence of specific obligations or reporting requirements." That is really a perfect set-up for me at the moment — I've just been laid off from my job after 7+ years with the company and am completely without specific obligations. There are some reporting requirements, but those are at the behest of the Department of Unemployment Insurance. Once the grant payments start rolling in, I'll set aside being on the dole and can always reopen my claim once the stipend runs out.

"Stipend" — it seems to be built around the word "spend," so maybe it has something to do with how I'm required to distribute the money to support the local economy? I'm just spit-balling here — once I see the cash deposited in my account, I'll allocate some of my intellectual activity into further researching the meaning

Again this year, the recipients come from a wide variety of backgrounds — scientists, community activists, artists. Well, they seem to cast a pretty broad net for "artists"; I see a tap dancer and a puppeteer among the winners. I bet right now the puppeteer is berating himself for not tap dancing while dangling his marionettes, thinking he could have doubled his award. Another of the winners is a playwright. Now, this inspires me: I'm going to write a play about my quest to be nominated for a MacArthur grant. ~~If~~ When I win, that'll be so meta.

Maybe "stipend" is another word for a wire transfer? Or cashier's check? I hope the money comes soon so I can start to really dig into this.

There is a poet in this year's group, and part of why she was honored was because, in her latest work, she "abandons all punctuation." That seems like a pretty low bar that I could easily meet if not exceed with minimal effort dedication to my craft and without working up much of a sweat its good to have an aspirational goal still within reach

Well, as Shakespeare (who never won a genius grant, and his grasp of punctuation was pretty shaky) wrote: "What's past is prologue." While I'm not sure what that means, either, cutting and pasting it here has led to a moment of even greater creative inspiration: tap-dancing marionettes performing The Tempest. I just need to stage it in a suitably gritty, contemporary setting while working the themes of climate change and displaced peoples into the production. Sounds like a sure-fire 2016 winner to me!

I'll need a little help getting this underway so one of the anonymous MacArthur people can see my brilliant creativity in person. If you'd like to stipend me (am I saying that correctly?) I promise to reimburse you right after I'm featured in next year's announcement, especially since with this approach I'm likely to at least triple, if not quadruple, the usual payout. Talk about genius…

My Reign in MacArthur Grant Park
(October 11, 2017)

I'm starting to take this personally… the 2017 "genius grants" were just announced and once more — my name is nowhere to be found among the "24 extraordinarily creative people who inspire us all" and were named as "Fellows." I even did a Ctrl+F search on the MacArthur Foundation's website to make sure I hadn't skipped over my name in the press release.

I have some questions about this mysterious process:

- Why, in these gender-fluid times, are the recipients still referred to as "fellows?"
- In *The Washington Post*'s article about this year's grants, the award is described as "legendary for casting a spotlight upon relatively obscure academics, activists and artists." Gee, that describes me to a T — believe me, there is no artist more obscure on the face of this earth than Yours Truly. I've been blogging for five years and so far have seven followers. And two of them are alternate email aliases that I set up.
- How "relatively obscure" are the authors included in this year's honorees who have ALREADY been awarded a Pulitzer Prize? And a third who'd won a National Book Award? That's like being chosen Homecoming Queen AND Senior Class Valedictorian. Enough with the trophies, already.
- Another person received the award as recognition for work done as an "Immunologist." What's the big deal about that? I am immune to criticism, immune to poison

ivy, and — based on testimony I provided in a recent court case — immune from criminal prosecution (a pending civil trial is a separate matter). If I'd known such a quality could have led to my anonymous nomination, I would have leapt up from the stand and dramatically proclaimed, "You can't HANDLE the truth!"

- Would it have killed these MacArthur people to shoehorn just one more worthy recipient in their list of those "extraordinarily creative people who inspire us all?" I certainly think of myself that way... Well, perhaps I'm not "extraordinarily" creative (this is, after all, my second post regarding this oversight). And I may not "inspire" as much as "irritate." But I can state with 100% certainty that I qualify as a "people."

I am taking solace only in the fact that the amount of the grant has remained static since I last got my panties in a wad over this slight — the stipend is still a mere $625,000. No COLA, or at least an option to have it paid out in bitcoin? The money is subject to taxation, so that does take a bit of the gloss off the award.

But you know — I'm not in this (I'm speaking of the arts, just in case you were wondering) for the acclaim, or recognition, or prizes. I write because I am compelled to do so. It is my method of expression, my pathway to bliss, and my way of sharing — however modestly and inexpertly — my humorous take on our world so that others may derive some small measure of enjoyment from exposure to my thoughts.

And here's a thought: if I change my byline to "John Branning, a 501(c)(3) organization" — I think I can avoid any tax liability.

Pooh-Pooh Pulitzers
(April 16, 2019)

I've just completed a quick scan of the 2019 Pulitzer Prize winners and did not notice my name so immortalized. Bummer.

There are fourteen journalism categories and I didn't even make it to the finalist stage in any of them. Of course, the fact that I'm not a journalist may have played a part there.

My chances were perhaps better under "Letters, Drama & Music," which includes a number of brackets that are right in my wheelhouse:

- Fiction: When my wife comes home from work and asks me what I've been up to all day, I spin elaborate fictions to rival the greatest found in literature.
- Drama: Once I admit how I actually spent my day, drama ensues.
- History: The pathological need to camouflage and embellish my daily routine goes back decades.
- Biography: Just last week I asked a cashier at the grocery store how her day was going and she proceeded to tell me her life story. Wish I'd written it all down.
- Poetry: My movements around a tennis court have been described as "poetry in motion" – if by "poetry" one means free verse: obtuse and completely devoid of rhythm.
- General Nonfiction: Recognizing the popularity of both spiritual and medical tracts, I self-published my minimis opus – *I Know You're Up There Somewhere: The Story of Suppositories*.
- Music: This year's winner received the prize for her very first opera. I also composed my first opera (in a style best described as "bel can't-o"), entitled *Libretto-maine Poisoning*, in the key of E-coli. From the aria that opens Act II:

My gut took a lickin'
From undercooked chicken
I'm going through hell – wish
I'd passed on that shellfish
Mi dispiace
My face is all blotchy

Well… there's always 2020 to look forward to. I think I'll have a fighting chance under "Criticism" since I will be subjected to quite a bit of it after my wife finds out this is what I've been up to all day.

Brain on my Parade
(October 8, 2020)

I did not receive one of the MacArthur Foundation fellowships — colloquially known as a "genius grant" — in either 2015 or 2017; in those two years I felt I'd shown extraordinary originality in my creative pursuits along with a marked capacity for self-direction. Coincidentally, that's exactly the language the Foundation uses in its marketing materials. I can't believe such a prestigious institution would rip me off like that.

(In case you're wondering what happened in 2016, 2018, or 2019 — while I felt I'd continually shown extraordinary originality in my creative pursuits, I was likely disqualified in those years due to a marked capacity for self-delusion.)

Anyway – they named the 2020 recipients the other day and I, once again, am not among them. Well, that really sucks the big one. If anything, I drove myself to go <u>beyond</u> the mere "extraordinary" in my originality. Through the incorporation of techniques including visualization, mindfulness, and elimination of gluten from my diet, I achieved a level of originality that can only be described as "homicidal" since I really killed it this past year.

As far as my marked capacity for self-direction: I went to hell in a handbasket, all on my own, so I deserve a gold star in that category.

The fellowship comes with a $625,000 stipend, paid out over five years. Honestly, I'd prefer if the Foundation would pay it out all at once, since I'd like to be able to focus immediately on my creativity without the yoke of concern that weighs heavily upon me generated by my ~~lust for caviar~~ ~~my gambling addiction~~ ~~ransom demanded to squelch a sexting scandal~~ fervent desire to care for my family.

What, you may be asking, was the nature of the creative endeavor for which I felt ~~entitled~~ self-effacingly deserving of such recognition? While it's a little tricky to explain, let me see if I can dumb it down for you: I have been dedicating my spare time, of which I have a great deal, to developing a sociological approach to counseling the less fortunate among us regarding their various ~~annoying~~ pressing problems, as I remain firmly ensconced on the couch while offering my ~~unwelcome~~ insightful guidance. I plan to roll out this program under the name *Divan Intervention*™. Such a sizeable award would go a long way toward establishing the framework to take this concept national, right after I have a new settee delivered.

Speaking of dumbing things down… I'm surprised Donald Trump hasn't been tweeting on the heels of this announcement regarding his pique at being excluded from an award based on "genius." Here's a poem I just wrote about that:

> *I'm a genius (self-proclaimed);*
> *those MacArthur grants are LAME.*
> *Put that stipend on the table*
> *(I'll pay taxes when I'm able).*
> *Seems I'm one they should select,*
> *due to my great intellect.*
> *Here's a thought you might find zany:*
> *no one more than me is brainy.*

Well, absent yet another MacArthur grant there's always next year's Pulitzer Prize to look forward to. I'm very excited about my chances since I plan to compete for the Biography award by submitting my lightly-researched profile of Jared Kushner, entitled *The Son-in-Law Also Advises*. Any day now, I expect to receive Ivanka's ~~restraining order~~ blurb for the book jacket, and once... what's that? The deadline for submissions was last week?

Oh, crap... I guess I'll just scrounge together a few shekels from my meager savings and purchase a bigger handbasket.

Dissemblance of Things Past

Occasionally I'll reflect on a notable experience, benchmarking my development from childhood through all the stages leading to my current status of (im)mature adulthood.

Holy Molar
(February 21, 2015)

I'm recovering from a recent visit to the dentist to take care of a cavity lurking underneath an already-existing filling. That's like going into the assessor's office to pay your vehicle tax and coming out to find your car's been ticketed for an expired registration.

My first few childhood visits to the dentist were memorable. Perhaps "infamous" is the more appropriate adjective. One morning my dad said he would pick me up after school and we would "do something special together – it's a surprise!" I was beside myself with anticipation all day, telling classmates my dad and I were going on an adventure that afternoon. When the dismissal bell rang I ran to meet my dad and it was a surprise all right — we crossed the street and entered a dental office in the basement of a neighboring house. Dr. Smith was an energetic man with big hands and highly-corrected vision who initially overwhelmed me with his outsized persona. While I eventually became quite fond of him, his dexterity and visual acuity were… not ideally suited for his chosen profession. Many dentists craft jewelry as a hobby, a natural extension of their skill set. I think Dr. Smith pounded out anvils in his spare time.

While perhaps not at the top of his profession he was certainly competent, and I continued to see him until I graduated from high school, coinciding with his retirement. But back to that first visit: I sat in the waiting room, not really sure what to expect. A bear of a man wearing a white smock and thick glasses with an additional set of magnifying lenses attached poked his head through the doorway, saying, "C'mon back here with me, Big John!" I walked into the examination room with all its unsettling equipment: consoles with dials, devices attached to long hoses, the overhead light that always blinds you while being adjusted into position. Dr. Smith helped me into the long, contoured lounge chair and said he was going to take a look at my teeth to make sure they were healthy. He asked if that was OK with me and I nodded my head "Yes." He replied, "Great! Now let's open up," and I vigorously shook my head "NO." In the space of two seconds I decided to adopt an adversarial position for the remainder of the visit, refusing to open my mouth. He asked again, then cajoled, then insisted, then called my father into the room to help out. My dad grabbed my nose and chin to pry my jaw open so Dr. Smith could insert a clamp to prevent me from closing it again. Strangely, I made no attempt to escape the confines of the chair or office; I sat there throughout the entire ordeal but just refused to cooperate in any way.

After looking with the mirror and running the various picks around my teeth and gums, Dr. Smith removed the clamp, permitting me to again intractably clench my jaw shut. He noodled around behind me for a few moments and then told me to open up again. Those who don't learn from history are doomed to repeat it... After calling on my dad for another assist Dr, Smith prepared to x-ray my teeth. He inserted a holder with a small square of film attached into my forcibly-opened mandible and then told me to bite down. This was a poor choice of words since I nearly took his finger off when I did so.

During my most recent visit to the dentist it was time for that same "full series," and the modern method is truly out of science fiction; I stood stock-still at a mark on the floor while a series of cameras attached to flexible tracks traced trajectories all around my head. The x-ray machine Dr. Smith used all those decades ago, while no doubt state-of-the-art for its time, was still quite large and clunky to operate. A huge articulated arm dropped from the ceiling and held a radiation-generating head, about the size of a portable television set, with handles on either side to maneuver it into place, coming to a cone-shaped point on the side closest to my face. It looked like a space-age weapon to me. Then Dr. Smith said something regrettable: "I'm gonna shoot some x-rays." In the context of having this "weapon" pointed at my head, I understood him to say, "I'm gonna shoot a ray *gun*." I interpreted the unstated but implied outcome of this action to be "... in order to zap a gaping hole right through your little head."

He slowly worked the ungainly device closer and closer to the film holder; the nearer it got, the more panic-stricken I became. While zeroing in on the targeted spot, he unfortunately made contact with my face — the tip of the cone-shaped end brushed against my cheek. By that point my eyes could not bug any farther out of my head, so I communicated my fear in the only method left to me — I lurched to my left and vomited all over the floor. Dr. Smith stood there, surveying the scene. After exhaling a long breath he quietly said, "That's what the sink's for, son."

The release of fear via hurling had exhausted me, and I put up no further fight as he finished. The film indicated there were several cavities to deal with. As I continued to recline, flaccid and spent, I heard him tell my father: "He needs some fillings, Howard — but I just don't have it in me to do anything else with him today." We made an appointment to return in another week. Despite my abysmal behavior and the mess I'd made, Dr. Smith remained courteous and upbeat as I was leaving and directed me to his "treasure chest" — a collection of cheap plastic trinkets from which I could choose anything I wanted. This unexpected bounty completely changed my feelings about the whole experience; if only someone had told me this was the planned denouement before I'd climbed into the chair, I would have been much more complicit.

I came back the next week, excited by the prospect of getting to choose another toy when these "fillings" were over with. I sat back in the chair and when Dr. Smith asked me to "open up" I did so enthusiastically, unhinging my jaw so wide you could see clear down to my stomach. I was completely cooperative, opening and closing and turning this way and that right up until the moment he presented a needle full of Novocain that looked to be a foot long and started to jab at my tender gums. (This was before the practice of "pre-numbing" with a swab soaked in lidocaine.) Familiar with the look on my face, and how I expressed feelings of panic, he withdrew the needle and reminded me where the sink was. I managed to get past the fear that visit without further incident. However, right through my final visit with Dr. Smith many years later, I refused injections any time drilling was required.

At last week's appointment for the subterranean cavity removal, the dentist numbed me up real good (pre-numbing completely changed my feelings about needles); I was without feeling from ear to nose and jaw to left eyebrow. He applied the drill to my tooth and… I felt every bit of it. I'm fairly certain Dr. Smith's spirit was in the room that day, working through this new dentist to extract his revenge against me.

I know the correct phrase is exact revenge; I used "extract" in that previous sentence as a meager attempt at a play on words. But it does remind me of when I had all four of my wisdom teeth pulled during my college years and, for a brief moment, was convinced the oral surgeon had broken my jaw. I didn't know where the sink was in his office, either.

Making a Bee Line
(January 17, 2015)

Sammy Baum, from my second-grade class, had a birthday party that was the first boy-girl mixer I'd ever been to outside of mothers-with-toddlers get-togethers. Sam was a pretty smooth operator for an eight-year-old; a short, stocky kid with a preternaturally low, raspy voice — he sounded and acted with a maturity and self-assurance well beyond his tender years (imagine *SCTV*'s Eugene Levy in grade school). So, when it was time for Sammy's birthday blow-out, of course there were going to be ladies in attendance.

I recall about a dozen classmates at the party, evenly divided between guys and gals. It was a warm Saturday afternoon in late May, and Sammy's mother, quickly tiring of having us run rampant through her house, suggested we go across the street to an undeveloped lot to gallivant and release some of our cake-and-ice-cream-fueled energy while she stretched out on the couch with a damp washcloth covering her eyes. Without parental oversight we quickly divided along gender lines: the boys hung out together to throw stuff, and the girls formed a circle for some game involving chants and random frolicking. The property had a stream running through it — in reality, a culvert for storm runoff but in our minds it was a mighty river to explore. In the midst of our playing I suddenly heard a scream; I looked up and Andrea Goldberg was on the other side of the creek, shrieking and running for her life.

Andrea was tall (taller than me, anyway), with blue eyes and pale skin, and wore her fine blonde hair in what I imagined were Scandinavian braids. She was very smart, especially good at math. I loved her — we were going to get married and have four children together and she would invest our savings, a future of which she was not yet aware. As Andrea shrieked and ran past I felt compelled to rescue my damsel in distress. "I'LL SAVE YOU, ANDREA!" I cried out (those were my exact words), leaping into the water to ford my way across and offer my gallant assistance in the face of whatever had frightened her so. While the water was relatively shallow, I was not much more than four feet tall at the time and quickly sunk down nearly to my knees. Struggling through the muck at the bottom of the stream, one of my brand-new PF Flyers came off my right foot, forever surrendered to the murky depths. I emerged on the other side of the culvert with muddy trousers, a soaking wet shirt, and one foot clad only with a damp, floppy sock. But I remained focused on my mission and stumbled toward my beloved. "Andrea, are you OK?" She had stopped running by then, and when I spoke to her she turned to look at me with a broadening "Why are you talking to me?" look on her face. Another one of the girls — I don't recall whom because she was not my intended — explained that Andrea had been running from a bee, but the bee had flown off and Andrea didn't need some stupid boy's help anyway.

Now not only had I shed my shoe but also my dignity. By this time, Sammy's mother heard all the commotion, springing off the couch to come outside and see what the hell was going on across the street. She ordered us all back to the house and promptly made me remove my pants so she could rinse the mud off them. What's left to lose after being stripped of your dignity (and pants) — your will to live? I was now completely humiliated, not only in front of Andrea but all my classmates at the party. Sammy's mother called my mother to explain the situation, and shortly thereafter my mother showed up to take me home (rather than just bring me some dry clothes; Death, take me now…). My memory of events gets a bit hazy at this point; while I don't know for certain I left with tears in my eyes, I wouldn't be surprised if that were the case.

The school year ended several weeks later, and I didn't see Andrea again until the fall when we all returned to start third grade. She was in a different class that year — I only saw her on occasion in the hallway, or the lunchroom, or the playground (this is when "recess" used to be an essential part of the curriculum). She never spoke to me, nor I to her. I recall one time when she was huddled with her girlfriends on the playground and they all burst into laughter while stealing glances in my direction, which I imagined was the result of Andrea telling them about the time over the summer when that stupid boy over there was delusional and thought he was being heroic when he was just being a stupid boy.

Dear Andrea Goldberg: I may have been the one with soggy pants — but you were the one who was all wet. Hope you're happy with whatever fop you settled for and I trust he's being a good father to our children. And if by any chance you are now a financial planner — could you please give me a call?

Racked with Gelt
(December 23, 2014)

Like many Jewish children, I wanted to celebrate Christmas when I was little — strictly for the presents. While gifts were also a part of our family's Hanukkah tradition, they were doled out in what my younger self viewed as a parsimonious (I was a bright little fellow with a precocious vocabulary) fashion, only one per day. And I got stuff like: handkerchiefs. What seven-year-old carries a handkerchief, much less uses it for his snotty nose? That's what sniffling and, in a pinch, sleeves were for. My Christian friends received seemingly endless quantities of toys, games, bikes and motorized scooters, ski trips… goyim gift-getting overstuffed like a deli sandwich piled high with corned beef between two slices of irony. I wanted in.

I grew up in a reform (i.e., not so much "observant" as "nodding familiarity with") Jewish family, a sibling-free child of a Jewish mother and born-Christian-but-converted-to-Judaism-under-pressure-from-her-family father. When I entered elementary school, our neighborhood had a substantial Jewish population. I recall at least a quarter of my classmates being Jewish; there were enough that most classes went into a holding pattern during the celebrations of Rosh Hashanah and Yom Kippur since so many students were absent. I used to stay out for the first day of Rosh Hashanah but then plead to come in on the second since school was so much fun. Lots of arts and crafts, extended recess, no homework — much more education-casual than the norm. But midway through 5th grade we moved, and within my new school district there were a mere handful of Jewish families. By the time I reached high school, with over two thousand students attending Grades 10 through 12, less than a dozen Jews could be found amongst my classmates. "Excused absences" for the Jewish holidays meant a frantic effort to catch up on missed assignments, make-up tests, and the need to answer the same questions from my classmates every year: "Where were you?" — "What holiday is that?" — "Why can't you eat?" — "Where's your beanie?" A priest offered an invocation at my high school commencement, blessing all the graduates and their families "in the name of Our Lord and Savior, Jesus Christ." Hmm, I hadn't met this Christ fellow.

As I've gotten older I've become even less observant. My religiosity is akin to Elizabeth Warren's take on her purported Native American heritage: "I grew up with these stories about my family and always assumed they were true." I haven't been to temple for many years and usually lose track of when the Jewish holidays come around each year. As I type this I know we're in the middle of Hanukkah, but I'm not sure which night. As mentioned here, my wife and I are in a mixed marriage (she is level-headed and I am not), and neither of us did much in the way of introducing our son to either or, for that matter, any religion. My feelings about faith and organized religion are too complex to articulate here but I will say, even as someone who hasn't attended synagogue in a long time, I still identify with that part of my background. I don't trot out the "I'm Jewish! How dare you?!" card when convenient, but maintain sensitivity to the challenges of a life lived as part of a minority. While nearly everyone can come up with a hyphenate as part of their self-description (African-American; mentally-challenged; differently-abled), it dismays me when people who are clearly advocating from a position of privilege or their own self-interest adopt some fabricated minority status in order to claim oppression or discrimination against them or others in their class. "White Rights," "The War on Christmas," and "Every Word Out Of

Lena Dunham's Mouth Is Pure Genius" are examples; there is no more a war on Christmas today than there is peace in Iraq. And even within legitimate minority communities, there are those who seek to absolve themselves of any personal responsibility for their status or (in)actions through some other fractional distinction. It would be like me claiming I was "present-deprived" as a kid because of my "Christmas-negative" status.

But I digress (did I mention I'm also "attention-deficient"?). Besides the handkerchiefs, I also recall receiving Hanukkah gifts including:

- The soundtrack to *My Fair Lady*, that perennial children's favorite.
- A subscription to *Horizon* – a hard-cover, rather high-brow arts magazine ostensibly ordered in my name but just so my mother could read it.
- A remote-control car. Now, this sounds like *exactly* the kind of thing a young boy would be thrilled to get. This version, however, wasn't controlled by a radio remote but instead by a plastic bellows attached to a narrow tube running to the car; squeezing the bellows was supposed to change the car's direction. 1) It didn't. 2) The hose was only about three feet long, so I had to waddle along behind the car as it rolled aimlessly across the living room floor. 3) The batteries in the car lasted about 20 minutes and there were no replacement "C" batteries in the house, ever. I played with it for that brief period on one day and never again. (And yes, I recognize the "… and the portions are so small" contradiction here.)
- A pretend medical kit, the kind with a plastic stethoscope, a blood pressure cuff where the needle would spin wildly just like when your grandfather was having a stroke, a fake thermometer that ended up getting stuck in all kinds of places — a true classic toddler toy. The Hanukkah my parents gave this to me, I was fifteen years old.

I'd like to believe I've grown up into a generous person — not extravagant by any means, but not anywhere near as stingy or misdirected as my parents were when it comes to giving gifts. Certainly, our family is quite fortunate in that there's nothing we need and little we want. At this time of year, it seems more appropriate to be focused on what we can give to and do for others and not at all concerned with what we may receive.

There's really only one thing I ask: if someone could point me toward where I can get a decent corned beef sandwich up here in the middle of Maine… I mean, I've heard even Jesus grew up in a kosher household.

Recipe for Disaster
(June 16, 2014)

My mother was truly an abysmal cook, despite the fact that my grandmother was a wonder in the kitchen. Don't these kinds of skills typically get handed down in families — mother to daughter, father to son, or whatever other combination you can come up with, including extended, blended, or "I have two mommies/daddies" families?

Regardless — despite her lack of ability, my mother was blissfully unaware of her culinary deficiencies and in fact seemed to actually enjoy the process. When Carol and I were first married and would come to visit my parents for a weekend, my mother would greet us and then let us know, "I've been cooking for days!" She would say this with tremendous excitement, which would prompt a response of "Oh, great!" from us, along with furtive glances meaning, "What in the hell has she made NOW?"

Adding stereotypical insult to injury, my mother's side of the family is Jewish. Jewish mothers are supposed to be wonderful cooks, are they not? It's part of their overbearing nature to browbeat their children, especially their sons, with psychological, emotional, and caloric overload. My mom was up to par on the first two but not the last one. She would cook a brisket (there's a classic Jewish main course for you) for periods ranging from several days up to a week (hence her quite literal statement above), boiling it for a few hours, returning it to the refrigerator, and then repeating the process ad nauseam (again, literally). It resulted in a cut of meat that was not so much tender to the fork as separated into individual muscle fibers that could be twirled like spaghetti. This would be served with a side of carrots and onions that had suffered the same fate as the poor beef – all lingering firmness and flavor extracted and existing only as a gelatinous remnant of what they once were.

Now, some of you might be saying, "Hey, don't be so rigid and sexist in your evaluation — what about your dad? Couldn't he pick up some of the household responsibilities? Many fathers have excellent kitchen skills!" Yes, many do — but mine didn't. When I was in the 6th grade, my mother was in the hospital for several weeks. Every night she was away we had the same thing for dinner — frozen minute steaks, pound cake (which came in pre-cut slices), and (humorously) Dad's Root Beer to wash it all down. Some fathers are lost in the kitchen but know their way around a grill. Not mine — he only made hot dogs and hamburgers, always reeking of lighter fluid. How do you like your burger: rare, medium, well-done, or the way my dad made them — 20 minutes per side?

Other crimes my mother committed against food:

- She would burn Campbell's tomato soup. Every. Single. Time. (And she always made it with water, never with milk.)
- She would make stuffing from saltine crackers. Meaning, she would crumble saltine crackers and stuff them into the middle of… whatever.
- One of her specialties was "baloney casserole." Don't ask.

- She made chocolate chip drop cookies that had a strange sponge-y consistency and tasted slightly of lemon. The bargain-brand chocolate chips she used retained their original shape and shrapnel-like hardness since they were impervious to heat.
- She would place slices of processed American cheese atop a roasting chicken. The cheese would remain there the entire time that poor bird was in the oven, resulting in two blackened squares devoid of any vestige of edibility. As was the rest of the meal.

Interestingly (and some might say "Freudishly," if there were such a word to be said), I became very interested in cooking once I moved out of my parents' house. I would cook for my college roommates and often contributed to or entirely prepared meals when Carol and I started seeing each other. As with any dating couple, we occasionally went to each other's family's house for dinner. My mother asked me to invite Carol over one night, and when I told Carol about the request she was silent for a moment and then asked, tentatively, "What is your mother going to make?" It was clear that she could not stomach (literally) another bite of my mother's cooking, at least not at that stage in our relationship. I promised Carol I would work closely with my mother to come up with something edible. I found a recipe for chicken Florentine (on the box of saltine crackers!) and all but told my mother that was what we'd be having for dinner the night Carol was coming over. I ended up taking control in the kitchen and preparing the dish on my own. I brought the plates out to the dining room table and we sat down to eat. My mother refused to take one single bite of what I'd made. Did I mention our Jewish heritage? Guilt was a prominent ingredient in my mother's spice rack.

Several years after my mom died, my dad married a woman named Gloria, who was marginally better in the kitchen. She had a few stock recipes she would rotate through and most of them were at least edible. (Example: whole bone-in chicken breasts covered with a mixture of canned cranberry sauce and onion soup mix, baked a really long time until they were quite dry.) She often served a spinach salad with dinner, with sliced hard-boiled eggs in it. I have a life-long aversion to hard-boiled eggs (something I never remember my mother making; go figure), so I would gingerly steer my fork around the discs of yolk and albumin and pick out the more salad-y parts to eat. Not wanting to be difficult, I never asked her to make the salad without eggs and, despite always leaving them on my plate, she never did. Several years into their marriage, my dad was going to have major surgery and I spent a week visiting, making the ten-hour drive by myself, while he had the operation and until he was discharged. I stayed at Dad and Gloria's place and she made dinner every night I was there — always serving that spinach salad. I suspected she was trying to express something subliminally, perhaps thinking my visit expressed a lack of confidence in her ability to tend to my father. After the first few nights I didn't take any of the salad with my dinner. "You don't want any salad?" "No, thank you; just not that hungry tonight." The next evening when she brought dinner to the table, I declined to eat anything. "I don't have any appetite," I claimed. The following day I passed on breakfast and lunch as well. "Are you OK?" Gloria asked. "Is something wrong?" I said I was just concerned about my dad's condition (which was true) and was anxious for him to come home from the hospital (which was also true), and I imagined my emotional tumult had squelched my appetite (which was true only insofar as it involved any food Gloria put in front of me). If my mother and Gloria could use food as a weapon, then so could I. Never mind that I was only punishing myself since I was withering away without taking any sustenance.

My dad was discharged and came home, and I stayed for a couple more days to make sure he was settling in and Gloria was comfortable taking care of him. They got into their routine, so I drove back. I walked in the door at home that evening, greeted by the smells of a delicious dinner (did I mention Carol is a wonderful cook — as was her mother?). "Poor baby," Carol cooed. "After your long trip, you must be starving!" She didn't know the half of it. I told her I really hadn't eaten much of anything for the last few days. When she asked me why not... I really couldn't come up with an answer. I suddenly felt ashamed that I'd proved to be such a difficult guest in response to Gloria's hospitality, and felt foolish for thinking her menu choices were somehow designed to express resentment. In addition to the meal Carol was serving, I also had some food for thought.

Thank God there weren't any cheese slices melted on it.

Let's Face It
(December 13, 2014)

My dear friend Charlotte is in the midst of an around-most-of-the-world trip: her itinerary includes stops in Europe, Asia, Australia, South America and maybe even Poughkeepsie. She is occasionally meeting up with family and friends in various locations but is largely seeing two-thirds of the world on her own. She maintains a lively travel blog and recently wrote of traveling inward — spending time exploring solitude.

Charlotte describes herself as an extrovert, so consciously choosing to spend some portion of her time minimizing contact with other people and stimuli was challenging and ultimately rewarding. I, however, am quite the introvert. This might come as a surprise to those of you reading this who know me. Years ago I was part of a work team that completed personality assessments; we compared outcomes afterward, and when I said the test indicated I was an introvert most of the others expressed disbelief — "You're always joking around!" "You're so outgoing!" But one very perceptive co-worker looked at me and offered the correct analysis: "You're an introvert *posing* as an extrovert." Truer words were never spoken, other than "Don't order the seafood platter at Denny's." If we've ever had a dialogue or been together in a group activity, you've no doubt noticed how remarkably red-faced I become the moment I open my mouth. It doesn't matter what I have to say — something as simple as introducing myself will trigger a blush so profound that I'm frequently asked how I got so sunburned... in the middle of winter. It's embarrassing, making it self-perpetuating behavior — I say something, which gets me red-faced; I'm aware I'm blushing, which makes me even redder. Sometimes in photos my face is blurry when others are in focus because my head is throwing off so much heat. Unlike Charlotte, I embrace being by myself. When I used to travel for business, my wife would complain being alone in the house drove her nuts. Carol recently enrolled in a class that takes her out of town for one long weekend each month. I miss her while she's gone, but I look forward to being on my own, with only the cats as my companions. They share my aversion to conversation and don't care if I leave the dirty dishes until the next day.

I've spent a fair amount of my working life in roles where presentation was an essential part of the job — corporate training consumes much of my résumé, and other roles involved running demonstrations or leading meetings. I've always liked to believe I'm a good communicator and facilitator, reasonably articulate, and can manage the flow and interplay among participants well. Perhaps that's because I am uniting them with their collective amazement at how red my face is, their curiosity at how much redder it can possibly get, and even a touch of fear regarding their proximity if my head were to spontaneously combust and explode.

Please don't confuse my introversion with being anti-social. I do tend to shy away from large functions and am not much at striking up conversations with people I don't know. But if I spy some familiar faces at a big party or a stranger initiates a chat with me — I can be very loquacious and occasionally entertaining. But I inevitably hit a point where the well runs dry, and I go back to hugging the wallpaper, often leaving the function hours before its scheduled end. Once, I was a participant in a week-long training class of a dozen employees, most of whom I hadn't met before our session began. I sat quietly during the first two days, speaking only when spoken to. At the start of Day Three, I made a conscious decision to be more outgoing and initiate some discussion during our group breakfast. I smiled broadly when I entered the room, offering a boisterous "Good morning!" to all, and began to recount some anecdote, using sweeping gestures and giving dramatic voice to the narrative. Everyone was entranced, keeping their eyes focused on me throughout my "performance." I concluded my tale, and shortly afterward one of the session leaders came over and asked if she could speak with me for a moment. She took me by the arm and led me away from the larger group. She smiled and kindly said, "You've got something hanging from your nose." I grabbed a napkin and swiped at my face — dislodging a dried booger the size of a raisin. There wasn't another peep out of me for the rest of the week.

Since moving to the lake, I've been fortunate enough to work from home, keeping in touch with co-workers via various electronic methods. On one project I've been working with a team that has a daily video check-in; our webcammed faces joining a row at the top of the screen as we log in. When I'm added to the display, I see a cozy warm halo surrounding my head. I'd say it's almost Christ-like if I weren't Jewish. I guess that makes it more nebbish-like.

One day I hope to find myself completely at ease, able to let go of whatever angst is buried deep within that contributes to my introversion and discomfort in the spotlight. However, I suspect the only time I'll ever be completely at peace will be when I die — I'll make a milky-faced corpse when my brain is no longer wrestling with my anxieties.

Kind of ironic I've requested to be cremated.

Climb Every Mantra
(January 22, 2017)

Carol asked me the other day if I'd be interested in going to Kol Nidre with her that evening. I was confused by her request since: 1) it wasn't anywhere near Yom Kippur, and 2) Carol isn't Jewish. When I asked her to clarify the reason behind her inquiry, she said it would help us learn to focus and relax. Now I was completely flummoxed, so I turned down the TV, pulled out my earphones, stopped scrolling through Facebook on my phone, and stepped off the treadmill. "What exactly is it you want to do tonight?"

Once I was paying closer attention, I understood she was asking if I wanted to go to Yoga Nidra with her. Ah, OK — to the untrained ear, Aramaic and Sanskrit sound an awful lot alike. I was forced to admit I knew as much about Yoga Nidra as Carol knew about Kol Nidre, so I asked her to provide a brief explanation. She said it was a method of achieving deep relaxation; getting the mind and body into a state of consciousness between waking and sleeping. I said I wasn't sure why this was something that required practice since that's how I spend most of my days. She went on to clarify that the focus was more on achieving a "wakeful" state while still being very relaxed, and when one reaches such a condition the body rejuvenates, and the mind opens to profound insights. I said I wasn't sure this was all that different from attending Yom Kippur services, which also cultivated drowsiness while requiring you to remain attentive. Carol said the two were nothing alike and suggested once the Yoga Nidra session was done we could go out to eat. I said she was further proving my point; the highlight of the Day of Atonement is the meal when it's all over. But because I am open to new experiences and also because Carol gave me "that look" — I agreed to go with her.

Once we arrived at the yoga studio, I had to sign a release. "Release from what?" was my question; I had to agree I wouldn't hold the business liable for any injury that might occur during the session. I asked what kind of injury could possibly be inflicted while trying to achieve a state of deep relaxation while stretched out prone on a mat at floor level, unless I somehow managed to be lulled into an irreversible coma? Again, Carol gave me "that look," and I acquiesced and signed the paperwork. We ditched our shoes and I dropped my attitude.

This was a popular program; there must have been at least sixty people in the room. I wondered how anyone could achieve a state of deep relaxation in such a crowded, enclosed space. I thought perhaps the tight quarters combined with deep breathing would lead to elevated levels of CO_2, and therefore people were confusing profound insights with hallucinations brought on by oxygen deprivation. Now I was understanding why I had to sign that release.

The session got underway with several basic yoga poses focused on gentle stretching and alignment, which caused me to break into a sweat while fighting off foot cramps. About fifteen minutes in, we began to work on our state of consciousness. We lay still while listening to our instructor, a very knowledgeable and charming woman named Sagel, review the seven chocolates. There are *seven* kinds of chocolate? Let's see: there's Snickers, 3 Musketeers, Twix, KitKat, Mounds, Almond Joy... I was drawing a blank on the last one. I whispered to Carol on my left to ask if she knew, and she replied we were supposed to be focusing on the seven chakras. Well, Jesus — I could relax, or I could focus on chakras, but how could I possibly do BOTH AT THE SAME TIME?

I don't recall the specifics of the seven chakras because, in all honesty, by that point I was craving something sweet. Once we were done with the chakras, Sagel had us direct our focus on individual parts of the body: sections of the arm; the leg; the torso; head and neck... She named every appendage by name except for the tingly parts.

Next came instruction to focus on the breath flowing through each nostril, individually. I could pick out the left (I don't mean "pick" that way) but couldn't manage to isolate the right. Left-breathing is supposed to lower your blood pressure, while right-breathing raises it back up. The risk of lapsing into a coma was inching closer to reality.

Since the class had people ranging from novice to expert, Sagel said we should each do whatever we felt was necessary to relax. So... I got up and dashed into the pub next door for a quick beer. I would have slipped back into my spot unnoticed except for belching as I resumed my Savasana pose.

We completed the session after another thirty minutes. Sagel then guided our return to a "normal" state of awareness. Well, except for the woman who was on my right — she was sleeping like a baby. I kneeled down, gently putting a hand on her shoulder while leaning in close to her ear to say, "WAKE UP! IT'S OVER!!" Everyone rolled up their yoga mats, re-folded blankets, returned blocks to storage, and exuded a sense of calm and well-being. I have to admit — I enjoyed the session more than I thought I would, finding it very peaceful. I felt more centered than when I arrived and actually had an insight unearthed from deep in my subconscious which helped me resolve an issue that had been preying on my mind for much of the evening: the seventh chocolate is a Milky Way.

Namaste.

Here's Everything I Know About Wine in Five Minutes or (Much) Less
(April 5, 2017)

I recently retired and am making good use of the free time I've gained by ignoring the long list of home improvement projects I promised to undertake and instead deciding to become a wine expert. Or, to use the correct term, an **oenophile**. Let me share what I've learned so far.

The first thing I've learned is the proper pronunciation of that term is "EE-no-file" and not, as I have long thought, "oh-NOFF-phil-lee." But I don't want to cloak myself in a mantle of pretentiousness right off the bat, so I'll refer to myself and others who share my ~~elitist~~ in-depth interest as "winers."

Step One in my journey was to work on developing my pallet. In order to accomplish this, I drove over to the local lumber yard where a very helpful lumberphile clarified I likely meant *palate*. I thanked him for his assistance, got back in the car, and headed for the nearest department store, where I was certain I would find a palate in the Housewares department, next to the silverware.

There is a great deal of ceremony that accompanies the ~~pretention~~ presentation of a fine wine, starting with uncorking the bottle. Does the bottle have a cork, and is that cork natural or synthetic? The use of natural corks can lead to a condition called "cork taint," which means if the bottle is so afflicted then you tain't gonna serve that wine to nobody. However, these days more and more higher-end vintages are utilizing screw caps. Someone should design a cap making it easier for those with arthritis to open a bottle, like what you find on prescription vials from the pharmacy. Push down — slight turn — glug glug glug.

Some believe wine is improved by aerating it, which is the practice of introducing air into the wine. There are devices designed for this purpose, the use of which are recommended versus introducing wine into the air by hurtling a full glass across the room in a drunken rage.

A wine's dryness is associated with the amount of tannin in it. My evaluation of this characteristic is coming along very slowly since all I've been able to discern, in every bottle of wine I've opened so far, is its level of wetness. In an effort to improve my abilities here, I got back in the car and went to a local tannin salon. One hour and $60 later, I wasn't any better at making the distinction but did leave with a new-found appreciation for the importance of sunblock.

Wine has a language all its own. Actually, that's not true — winers use common English words in unique and innovative ways to describe the characteristics of the fermented grape. In this context, adjectives like "angular," "opulent," and "fallen over" (which is what my wife Carol says happens after I finish my second glass) take on alternative meanings. One surprising designation is "stemmy," since I've always thought Stemmy was the late, great frontman for Motörhead. A wine can be described as "chewy;" I, for one, would certainly return any bottle of wine where I had to chew what poured out of it. After delighting in a recent tasting, I told Carol I'd enjoyed a Barbera with great legs that I'd found firm, musky, and voluptuous. She immediately filed for divorce, naming "Barbera" as the co-respondent.

I could go on but I've already spent enough time away from my studies. Tonight's lesson plan is to spend the evening exploring a companion I hope to find elegant, supple, and a bit racy. And if it turns out Carol has to work late, I'll just move on to a third glass and enjoy ~~tripping~~ ~~tipping~~ tippling on my own.

Live Forever or Diet in the Attempt
(March 15, 2018)

Lately, I've been trying to increase my exercise and decrease my daily caloric intake, after years of approaching these activities from the other direction. I'm doing reasonably well with the diet – smaller portions, avoiding seconds, and cutting out dessert (mostly). My weakness is my sweet tooth, so I made a vow at the start of the new year that I'd permit myself ice cream or cookies only once a week and on birthdays. Initially, I struggled with this since it's somebody's birthday nearly every day, innit?

The exercise has been the bigger challenge because I am essentially an immobile person. If I could afford it, I'd pay someone to grab me by the ankles and move my legs in a simulacrum of jogging while I remained seated on the couch watching *Law & Order* reruns. Of course, that's a very impractical idea since this approach would likely block my view of the TV.

I saw a report on the news the other night, discussing the results of a long-term study showing a connection between increased levels of exercise and decreased incidences of dementia. To obtain the data, researchers in Sweden followed a group of women for forty-four years; don't they have anti-stalking laws in Scandinavian countries? Regardless – the recommendation was that 150 minutes of cardiovascular exercise per week was the required amount to stave off… uh, what was I talking about?

I've gone through a variety of exercise equipment over the years – a treadmill, an elliptical machine, a NordicTrack. Like most people, I started out as an enthusiastic user but eventually got tired of the repetitive activity. "Why don't you just join a gym, where there are a variety of machines at your disposal?" you might ask me if I could remember who you are. Well, first of all – I'm a cheap bastard and gyms cost money. Also, I don't like to get undressed in front of anybody who is not my wife, a close blood relative, or possibly a supermodel. Third, hot fudge sundae.

At the present moment (sidebar: all moments are in the "present"), I've got my road bike (the tires of which have rarely touched pavement) attached to a stand that converts it into a stationary bike (which is essentially what it was, anyway). I've got it set up in the bedroom, positioned in front of the patio doors that lead to the deck, so I have a clear view of the backyard and the lake we live adjacent to. The view is captivating, regardless of the season, and I keep up my momentum by pedaling along to a playlist of high-energy songs on my iPod. I manage to work up a pretty good sweat, and that's just from properly adjusting the height of the bike seat.

I'm ten weeks into the new regimen and am certainly feeling better – although I haven't lost as much weight as I'd hoped. But, as they say: it's the journey, not the destination. Which doesn't make much sense, since I'm already *at* my destination because I'm riding a stationary bike. But the view is lovely, and I must remember to thank whoever lives in this house for letting me exercise in their bedroom.

Jest the Facts
(June 11, 2022)

Recently, I did something foolish.

Well, let me expand upon that statement: I have done many foolish things in my life, and thought I'd take this opportunity to tell you about the most recent one.

Now, when I say "most recent" – this is a bit like trying to explain the Heisenberg Uncertainty Principle. I can provide you with a long list of foolish things I've done and tell you when I did them, but that's not to say by the time I finish telling you about a past foolish incident that I won't have already laid the groundwork for the *next* foolish thing I am inevitably about to do.

I should look at my history of foolishness not as a random series of discreet incidents but as a continuum interrupted by only the briefest moments of aptitude and/or sheer luck.

I came into this world a fool and I'll exit it the same. As the noted philosopher G.W. Bush once proclaimed: "Fool me once, shame on – shame on you. Fool me… You can't get fooled again." And yet, again and again, I have either gotten fooled or fooled myself into thinking I'd achieved something worthwhile or unique – only to find out it was neither. Much like "W" himself.

"A fool and his money are soon parted." I'm reminded of this proverb every month when I look at the credit card statement.

"He who knows and knows that he knows is a wise man – follow him; he who knows not and knows not that he knows not is a fool." This was said by either Confucius or Donald Rumsfeld; I knows not which.

The Beatles sang mournfully about a "fool on the hill" who "sees the sun going down / and the eyes in his head / see the world spinning round." Why did they feel it necessary to specify this fool's eyes are "in his head"? Where else would they be located? Or were McCartney and Lennon picturing Mr. Potato Head whilst writing this tune, exercising poetic license to focus on just two of his many eyes?

Hmm… I think I've strayed from my original premise.

And illustrated my point.

List Less

I like to take common sayings, famous quotes, trite aphorisms, etc. and mock the sentiments expressed within them. Here are entirely too many of these things:

Aphorism Schism
(November 6, 2013)

A bird in the hand means I'll not be exchanging high-fives with you any time soon.

Keep your friends close and your enemies can eliminate all of you at once.

Those who don't learn from history are doomed to repeat the tenth grade.

Three things cannot be long hidden: the sun, the moon, and that stain on the carpet.

It is better to light a single candle than to curse the darkness. But who can find a candle when you bang your shin on the way to the bathroom in the middle of the night?

The definition of insanity is doing the same thing over and over again and you put something in my coffee, didn't you?

A journey of a thousand miles begins with a dead cellphone.

Two roads diverged in a wood, and I took the one less traveled by, and I got so fucking lost.

It does not matter how slowly you go as long as you're not in front of me on the expressway.

By believing passionately in something that does not yet exist, we keep those online dating services in business.

Fortune favors the brave. I guess that's why I fear trying to balance my checkbook.

A man's reach should exceed his grasp, or what's a step-ladder for?

Some see things as they are and ask, "Why?" I dream things that never were and ask, "Does Ambien have the same effect on you?"

Chance favors the prepared mind. What just happened?

Many people die at twenty-five and aren't buried until they're seventy-five. No wonder it's been so quiet around here.

It's not what you start in life, it's what you finish. Like that time wh

Many men go fishing their entire lives not knowing it is not fish they are after. Instead, they should have been on the lookout for double-negatives.

A chain is only as strong as its weakest link. That's why Circuit City went out of business.

There is only one way to avoid criticism: do nothing, say nothing, and be nothing. OK, I guess there are three ways to avoid criticism.

What we see depends on what we look for. I'm looking for trouble, and right now I see you.

I try. I fail. I try again. The day is shot.

We are what we imagine ourselves to be. What we really are is just too damn depressing to contemplate.

Bitter Patter
(April 6, 2014)

Looks can be deceiving. Smell, however, should be trusted implicitly.

It's not what you know, it's who the hell told you??

Pride goeth before a fall. That's why I stick to the couch.

One man's meat is another man's poison. That's why you should avoid the Beef Stroganoff at any luncheonette.

I cried because I had no shoes. Then the salesman came out with a size 10 wide and I was happy.

Give me your tired, your poor, your huddled masses yearning to breathe free, the wretched refuse of your teeming shore. No, wait — on second thought, you can keep the wretched refuse.

If you can't stand the heat, get out of the sauna.

Who knows what evil lurks in the heart of men? Their ex-wives know.

The wages of sin is death, but they do offer a 401(k) match.

The man who has confidence in himself gains the confidence of others. At least that's what my financial advisor told me as I handed him that check.

If not us, who? If not now, when? No, next week is bad for me.

He who hesitates is lost. But he'll never ask for directions, that's for sure.

Ask me no questions and I'll tell you no lies. I guess that doesn't leave us much to talk about.

A little knowledge is a dangerous thing. I like to live dangerously.

A prophet is not recognized in his own land. Check again, I'm sure my name's on the list.

Good things come to those who wait. Yes, that's the same thing I told you yesterday.

Lightning never strikes twice in the same place, so slide over a little.

Many a true word is spoken in jest. You are stupid and ugly, LOL.

There is many a slip 'tween cup and lip, particularly after last call.

You can catch more flies with honey than vinegar, but really — could you just close the screen door behind you?

Adage Before Beauty
(October 28, 2014)

When someone talking to you says "long story short", it's already too late.

Know how I play "Words with Friends"? By cursing at them.

There but for the grace of God go I. Plus there was a *Breaking Bad* marathon on TV.

It's said, "All politics is local." That's incorrect; it should be, "All politics are insulting to the electorate."

I've begun a new exercise regimen. So far, I'm exercising my right not to follow it.

When I was a young camper I was once thrown from a horse. Now when someone asks if I'll ever saddle up again I say, "Neigh."

Avoid trying anything labelled as "new & improved" since it is likely neither.

I roasted a chicken the other night. I hope it understood my zingers were offered in jest.

Any cocktail made with more than 4 ingredients (including ice) is just not worth the effort.

What do you get when you cross a duck with a hornet's nest? You get one pretty pissed-off duck, for starters.

I fell off a ladder and through the roof. Not surprisingly, I broke out in shingles.

A man is known by the company he keeps. Please go home now.

I beat the rap on a charge of home invasion by claiming I was participating in the new "sharing economy".

An injury is sooner forgotten than an insult. That's why I kicked you, jackass.

None of us is as smart as all of us. But I is much smarter than you is.

The night has a thousand eyes. "Mississippi" runs a close second.

Goal all the Way
(December 8, 2015)

Success is the ability to go from one failure to another with no loss of enthusiasm. – Winston Churchill

- No wonder Churchill was in politics, since that kind of attitude got me dismissed from several prior positions in the "real world."

The obstacle is the path. – Zen saying

- Turn around and head back to the car. – Just saying.

Whenever you see a successful person, you only see the public glories, never the private sacrifices to reach them. – Vaibhav Shah

- And aren't we all thankful for that?

Success? I don't know what that word means. I'm happy. But success, that goes back to what in somebody's eyes success means. For me, success is inner peace. That's a good day for me. – Denzel Washington

- I like Denzel as much as the next guy, but he should stick to a script.

Opportunities don't happen. You create them. – Chris Grosser

- Hence some unverifiable entries on my résumé.

A successful man is one who can lay a firm foundation with the bricks others have thrown at him. – David Brinkley

- I don't believe our local building codes permit this.

No one can make you feel inferior without your consent. – Eleanor Roosevelt

- These affirmative consent guidelines on college campuses are really getting out of hand.

Don't be afraid to give up the good to go for the great. – John D. Rockefeller

- Rockefeller made his fortune scooping up all those abandoned goods at rock-bottom prices.

If you can't explain it simply, you don't understand it well enough. – Albert Einstein

- Oh, I understand it perfectly — it's my boss who's no Einstein.

There are two types of people who will tell you that you cannot make a difference in this world: those who are afraid to try and those who are afraid you will succeed. – Ray Goforth

- There are actually three types of people but I'm afraid to tell you about the third one.

Start where you are. Use what you have. Do what you can. – Arthur Ashe

- Canadian doubles is for sissies.

It is necessary for us to learn from others' mistakes. You will not live long enough to make them all yourself. – Hyman George Rickover

- But, in my case, not for lack of effort.

Any activity becomes creative when the doer cares about doing it right, or better. – John Updike

- Any activity becomes better when it includes Dewar's and soda.

Be wiser than other people, if you can; but do not tell them so. – Philip Dormer Stanhope

- What if I say I received "anonymous complaints" that they're all dumb as rocks?

The bravest are surely those who have the clearest vision of what is before them, glory and danger alike, and yet notwithstanding go out to meet it. – Thucydides

- I'm happy to be certified as second-tier brave and just go out to meet the glory.

Fortune favors the brave. – Terence

- I'll settle for a 60/40 split if you'll handle all the danger stuff.

One of the lessons of history is that nothing is often a good thing to do and always a clever thing to say. – Will Durant

- "   !"

The speed of a runaway horse counts for nothing. – Jean Cocteau

- Unless you're the horse.

The cure for boredom is curiosity. There is no cure for curiosity. – Ellen Parr

- A fatal diagnosis if you're a cat.

All good things which exist are the fruits of originality. –John Stuart Mill

- That's great, since I hate vegetables.

You'll always miss 100 percent of the shots you don't take. – Wayne Gretzky

- Hasn't this been adopted as the motto of the NRA?

The dreadful burden of having nothing to do. – Nicolas Boileau

- Here's something to keep you busy — try writing complete sentences.

I learned much from my teachers, more from my books, and most from my mistakes. – Anonymous

- Mistake #1 – forgetting to sign his name to this insight.

A wise man will make more opportunities than he finds. – Sir Francis Bacon

- Breakfast irony: one can never make enough bacon.

Measure twice, cut once. – Craftsman's aphorism

- Count your fingers immediately afterward.

If I have seen further than others, it is by standing upon the shoulders of giants. – Sir Isaac Newton

- Admittedly, at the risk of pissing off the giants.

I not only use all the brains that I have, but all that I can borrow. – Woodrow Wilson

- You weren't using yours, anyway.

A good solution applied with vigor now is better than a perfect solution applied 10 minutes later. – George S. Patton

- If this were true then I wouldn't have participated in so many exit interviews.

Clear your mind of can't. – Solon

- Screw you, Solon. — Kant

My Search for Happiness (on Google)
(June 20, 2017)

For every minute you are angry you lose sixty seconds of happiness. — Ralph Waldo Emerson

- But for every day you are angry, you can probably get out of making dinner.

Happiness is when what you think, what you say, and what you do are in harmony. — Mahatma Gandhi

- Misery is when people insist on harmonizing about how happy they are.

Happiness is a warm puppy. — Charles M. Schulz

- Right up until the moment when something else warm comes out of that puppy.

When one door of happiness closes, another opens, but often we look so long at the closed door that we do not see the one that has been opened for us. — Helen Keller

- I presume she was speaking figuratively here.

A table, a chair, a bowl of fruit and a violin; what else does a man need to be happy? — Albert Einstein

- And so Einstein put rumors of his affair with Marilyn Monroe to rest.

Life is really simple, but we insist on making it complicated. — Confucius

- So true — in addition to the original cereal, you can now buy Life in Cinnamon, Vanilla, and Pumpkin Spice.

I'd far rather be happy than right any day. — Douglas Adams

- But it's tough to keep your chin up when the boss insists you're wrong every single day.

Everyone wants to live on top of the mountain, but all the happiness and growth occurs while you're climbing it. — Andy Rooney

- For those who remember Andy Rooney, he looked like he never climbed a set of stairs — much less a mountain.

That man is richest whose pleasures are cheapest. — Henry David Thoreau

- Try telling that to my wife when I suggest we go to Arby's on date night.

A well-developed sense of humor is the pole that adds balance to your steps as you walk the tightrope of life. — William Arthur Ward

- And also helps you tolerate extended metaphors.

Happiness consists of living each day as if it were the first day of your honeymoon and the last day of your vacation. — Leo Tolstoy

- Makes you wonder why his best-known novel wasn't published under the title, *Sex and Booze*.

In the midst of movement and chaos, keep stillness inside of you. — Deepak Chopra

- Which is why I'm refusing to get up from the couch to unload the dishwasher.

The right way is not always the popular and easy way. Standing for right when it is unpopular is a true test of moral character. — Margaret Chase Smith

- Oh, how the body politic has changed.

If you hear a voice within you say, 'You cannot paint,' then by all means paint and that voice will be silenced. — Vincent van Gogh

- Not if you don't spread a drop cloth and spackle the walls first.

Our greatest happiness does not depend on the condition of life in which chances placed us, but is always the result of a good conscience, good health, occupation, and freedom in all just pursuits. — Thomas Jefferson

- Compare Jefferson's erudition to this tweet:

Songs of Romance and Passion, Updated
(November 29, 2017)

To all the girls I've loved before / I thought I was pursuing shared feelings, even though I now realize I was mistaken.

Pour some sugar on me, C'mon, fire me up / Really — every woman who wants to join my staff has to do it.

You say it's urgent / Make it fast, make it urgent / Do it quick, do it urgent / Gotta rush, make it urgent / I have to get back on the Senate floor for a roll call vote in 5 minutes.

Do that to me one more time / So I can surreptitiously tape it as proof to hand over to the Ethics Committee.

In a restaurant, holdin' hands by candlelight / While I'm touchin' you, wanting you with all my might, ooh / Don't worry — my wife is back in the district with our kids and never comes to DC.

I've been taking on a new direction / But I have to say / I've been thinking about my own protection / But you're still using birth control, right?

Voulez-vouz coucher avec moi, ce soir? / Wait — I never asked if you'd sleep with me; I thought I was just asking you in a cute way to bring some papers over to my apartment.

I got tired of waiting, wondering if you were ever coming around / My faith in you was fading, when I met you on the outskirts of town / Because you said you couldn't pick me up at my house due to the difference in our ages.

Dim all the lights, sweet darlin' / I don't want anyone from the mainstream leftwing socialist Democrat news media to catch us.

Oh she may be weary / Them young girls they do get wearied / But the age of consent in Alabama is 16, so I've got nothing to worry about.

Sometimes you picture me, I'm walking too far ahead / You're calling to me, I can't hear what you've said / I said, "Congressman, what is your response to the latest allegations?"

I hope you don't mind, I hope you don't mind, that I put down in words / A non-disclosure agreement I want you to sign first.

You're asking me will my love grow — I don't know, I don't know / Oh, here's the Viagra — it's all good.

Not If I CPU First
(April 3, 2019)

We disabled cookies on our home computer since we're trying to lose weight.

Security experts recommend using only secure WiFi networks so I glued our router to the countertop.

I bought an external hard drive but can't find a cord long enough to reach the computer from outside.

I don't find it necessary to clear the cache since my wife routinely empties my wallet.

Do I need to install anti-virus software if I already got a flu shot?

I'd be happy to back up my data but so far it hasn't asked for my support.

I wanted to use a thumb drive but my wife insisted I keep both hands on the steering wheel at all times.

Another recommendation is to scan for spyware so I checked: I own neither a fedora nor a trench coat.

I bought a surge protector yet was still charged three times the normal fare last time I used an Uber.

I wasn't sure how to activate the firewall so instead stuck a smoke detector on the back of the monitor.

I'd love to upgrade my operating system but suppose I should finish medical school first.

It took some effort to convince my wife that "removing malware" did not mean she could get rid of all those Tommy Bahama shirts in the back of my closet.

Pro tip: don't attempt to clean your keyboard by running it through the wash. Even if there's a "Delicates" setting.

My son asked if he could get a wireless mouse; I replied not until you prove you can take care of it responsibly.

I've never understood the purpose of re-booting your computer since it seems like it would be pretty much useless after you kicked it the first time.

I decided against purchasing a touchscreen monitor because I wasn't comfortable signing the consent form that came with it.

How do you know if your credit card information is secure when making an online purchase? Oh, you'll find out in about 10 minutes.

I heard a very funny joke about the Apple MacBook but won't repeat it here – it's not PC.

Philosophers Stoned
(April 16, 2018)

There is nothing permanent except change. — Heraclitus

- So true — I've been walking around with one of those $1 Sacagawea coins in my pocket for, like, three months now.

Let us sacrifice our today so that our children can have a better tomorrow. — A. P. J. Abdul Kalam

- Only because society frowns on those who sacrifice their children.

It is better to be feared than loved, if you cannot be both. — Niccolo Machiavelli

- And if you can, then throw "… and really rich" into the mix.

Learning never exhausts the mind. — Leonardo da Vinci

- Then why do teachers look so drained at the end of the school day?

The only journey is the one within. — Rainer Maria Rilke

- The only tedious journey is the one within a bus.

Think in the morning. Act in the noon. Eat in the evening. Sleep in the night. — William Blake

- When am I supposed to binge-watch *Game of Thrones*?

It is far better to be alone, than to be in bad company. — George Washington

- Especially once they started touring on the same bill with Lynyrd Skynyrd.

Being entirely honest with oneself is a good exercise. — Sigmund Freud

- I avoid exercise. Honest.

Not all those who wander are lost. — J. R. R. Tolkien

- Some of them are just trying to find a restroom.

Tell me and I forget. Teach me and I remember. Involve me and I learn. — Benjamin Franklin

- And then — it's time for you to go home already.

Wise men speak because they have something to say; Fools because they have to say something. — Plato

- Where does compulsive tweeting fit into this?

Life is not a problem to be solved, but a reality to be experienced. — Soren Kierkegaard

- Sorry, I was scrolling through Facebook on my phone — what did you say?

The unexamined life is not worth living. – Socrates

- The examined life generally doesn't stand up to close scrutiny, either.

Entities should not be multiplied unnecessarily. – William of Ockham

- Good advice if you want to avoid having your taxes audited.

The life of man (in a state of nature) is solitary, poor, nasty, brutish, and short. – Thomas Hobbes

- I think Hobbes meant to say this about life in the state of Kentucky.

He who thinks great thoughts, often makes great errors. – Martin Heidegger

- For the rest of us thinking merely mediocre thoughts, there's spell check.

We live in the best of all possible worlds. – Gottfried Wilhelm Leibniz

- That's like saying I came in first out of a field of one.

God is dead! He remains dead! And we have killed him. – Friedrich Nietzsche

- On the bright side, this frees up your Sunday mornings.

There is but one truly serious philosophical problem, and that is suicide. – Albert Camus

- Mostly because it's very difficult to share any insights gained once committing it.

One cannot step twice in the same river. – Heraclitus

- But that pile of dog poop right in the middle of the sidewalk…

To be is to be perceived. *(Esse est percipi.)* – Bishop George Berkeley

- To pee is to be relieved. *(Esse est perpipi.)*

Liberty consists in doing what one desires. – John Stuart Mill

- John Stuart Mill, earliest casualty of the #MeToo movement.

Even while they teach, men learn. – Seneca the Younger

- Mostly, they learn they aren't paid enough for going into teaching.

There is only one good: knowledge, and one evil: ignorance – Socrates

- Somewhere in the middle of those two is the sweet spot.

One cannot conceive anything so strange and so implausible that it has not already been said by one philosopher or another. – René Descartes

- It's like I always say: one cannot conceive anything so strange and so implausible that it has not already been said by one philosopher or another.

There is only one thing a philosopher can be relied upon to do, and that is to contradict other philosophers. – William James

- Not true!

The mind is furnished with ideas by experience alone. – John Locke

- End tables and accent lighting not included.

Life must be understood backward. But it must be lived forward. – Søren Kierkegaard

- But when life goes sideways, you're on your own.

Metaphysics is a dark ocean without shores or lighthouse, strewn with many a philosophic wreck. – Immanuel Kant

- Metaphorically speaking.

Philosophy is at once the most sublime and the most trivial of human pursuits. – William James

- I guess he's never watched *Keeping Up With The Kardashians*.

He who is unable to live in society, or who has no need because he is sufficient for himself, must be either a beast or a god. – Aristotle

- Couldn't he just be a grouchy sort?

All that is necessary for the triumph of evil is that good men do nothing. – mistakenly attributed to Edmund Burke

- Burke didn't say this? Does that mean I have to do something else to ensure the triumph of evil?

Is man merely a mistake of God's? Or God merely a mistake of man's? – Friedrich Nietzsche

- The important thing to remember is that somebody screwed up somewhere.

I would never die for my beliefs because I might be wrong. – Bertrand Russell

- You, however, should go right ahead and jump off that cliff.

Happiness is the highest good. – Aristotle

- But a corned beef sandwich is a close second.

Man is condemned to be free. – Jean-Paul Sartre

- And I am free to condemn Sartre.

I don't know why we are here, but I'm pretty sure it is not in order to enjoy ourselves. – Ludwig Wittgenstein

- Every party has a pooper, that's why we invited you…

That man is wisest who, like Socrates, realizes that his wisdom is worthless. – Plato

- Ooh, burn!

If you would be a real seeker after truth, it is necessary that at least once in your life you doubt, as far as possible, all things. – René Descartes

- I'm not sure about this.

Happiness lies in virtuous activity, and perfect happiness lies in the best activity, which is contemplative. – Aristotle

- Lends credence to the rumors that Aristotle was asexual.

I can control my passions and emotions if I can understand their nature. – Spinoza

- I bet no one ever got a Valentine's Day card from this guy.

It is wrong always, everywhere and for everyone, to believe anything upon insufficient evidence. – W. K. Clifford

- Hear that, Fox News watchers?

The only true wisdom is in knowing you know nothing. — Socrates

- Then I must be the wisest man on the face of the planet.

We are too weak to discover the truth by reason alone. – St. Augustine

- In that case, let's order a pizza.

Making a Demi-Glace of Myself
(July 31, 2019)

I forgot to make pancakes for my son on his birthday. I feel waffle about it.

Did you know you can cook salmon in the dishwasher? It comes out better if you wrap it in foil first.

I tried making avocado toast but, even after removing the pit, I couldn't get either half into the toaster slot.

You can use panty hose instead of cheesecloth to strain foods. I do, however, recommend waiting until your wife takes them off.

The best way to prepare Brussels sprouts is to be direct with them: death is part of nature's cycle, and it's O.K. to be sad.

I wanted to try cooking some pork chops using a sous vide, but couldn't afford one – so I substituted a rectal thermometer. Unfortunately, I rectum.

I poached an egg and boy did the diners in the next booth give me what for.

A sure-fire way to dice an onion without tears is to have someone else do it.

You can grill a steak but may get a better outcome by asking a series of open-ended questions.

It's said that boeuf bourguignon is one of the most time-consuming dishes to prepare. No kidding – it took me 3 hours of trying to spell it correctly just to Google a recipe.

Someone told me a tomato is actually a fruit. I responded by telling them that term is antiquated and offensive.

I told my wife I wanted to spatchcock a chicken and she kicked me out of the house.

I attempted to embrace a plant-based diet. Unfortunately, the plant I chose to embrace was poison ivy.

When it comes to Swiss chard – I remain neutral.

I bought a candy thermometer. It was crunchy, but not very sweet.

My bartender told me in order to make a mojito, you should muddle the mint and lime. So I showed them the series finale of *Lost*.

Senior Winces
(March 6, 2022)

I turned 65 earlier this year, and this is my motto: *Age ain't nothing but a number of things going wrong, simultaneously.*

Life's tragedy is that we get old too soon and wise too late. – Benjamin Franklin

- Sadly, I became wise too late that I should have stopped watching *Killing Eve* after the first season.

No, that is the great fallacy: the wisdom of old men. They do not grow wise. They grow careful. – Ernest Hemingway

- No, the great fallacy is that old men think using hair dye will make them look younger.

Anyone who keeps the ability to see beauty never grows old. – Franz Kafka

- Okay, okay… you've talked me into getting that cataract surgery.

For the unlearned, old age is winter; for the learned, it is the season of the harvest. – Hasidic saying

- I have learn-ed I'm too old to participate in the season of the harvest, due to my arthritis and whatnot.

Wrinkles should merely indicate where smiles have been. – Mark Twain

- Dentures serve a similar purpose.

Today is the oldest you've ever been, and the youngest you'll ever be again. – Eleanor Roosevelt

- And yet I still can't keep track of what day of the week it is… Damn this pandemic.

Old age is an excellent time for outrage. My goal is to say or do at least one outrageous thing every week. – Louis Kronenberger

- This fellow never heard of "cancel culture."

Grow old along with me! The best is yet to be, the last of life, for which the first was made. – Robert Browning

- Is this, like, a roommate situation? Or does he have an in-law apartment set up at his place?

The old are in a second childhood. – Aristophanes

- Hence the market for adult diapers.

There is this difference between the grief of youth and that of old age: youth's burden is lightened by as much of it as another shares; old age may give and give, but the sorrow remains the same. – O. Henry

- O. Brother…

Man, like the fruit he eats, has his period of ripeness. Like that, too, if he continues longer hanging to the stem, it is but a useless and unsightly appendage. – Thomas Jefferson

- What's hanging from my stem has indeed become a useless and unsightly appendage.

In youth all doors open outward; in old age all open inward. – Henry Wadsworth Longfellow

- And don't even get me started on revolving doors.

Discern of the coming on of years, and think not to do the same things still; for age will not be defied. – Francis Bacon

- I defy you to parse that sentence.

After a man passes sixty, his mischief is mainly in his head. – Edgar Watson Howe

- Obviously – an insight gained before the introduction of Viagra.

No man loves life like him that's growing old. – Sophocles

- Should that read "like him" or "like he"? Grammar is, like, Greek to me.

White hair often covers the head, but the heart that holds it is ever young. – Honoré de Balzac

- The only thing my heart is capable of holding onto requires that I take a statin every day.

The habits of a young man are, like his coat, removable; the habits of an old man are like the drapery of a statue. – Austin O'Malley

- My habits are like when you get a sweater stuck over your head while trying to take it off.

Most fatal diseases had their own specific odor, but … none was as specific as old age. – Gabriel García Márquez

- Gee… I don't smell anything.

Old age is the most unexpected of all things that happen to a man. – Leon Trotsky

- Well, I honestly think the most unexpected of all things was when the Atlanta Falcons blew a 28-3 lead and lost in OT to the New England Patriots in Super Bowl LI.

Age seldom arrives smoothly or quickly. It's more often a succession of jerks. – Jean Rhys

- Much like everyone who has so far indicated their interest in the 2024 GOP presidential nomination.

Every age has a keyhole to which its eye is pasted. – Mary McCarthy

- Voyeurism is creepy at best, and a misdemeanor at worst.

In youth we learn; in age we understand. – Marie von Ebner-Eschenbach

- Understand what?

Rhymes A-Wastin' (Part I)

Out of the 600-plus Trump (and other politicos) poems I wrote, here's just a smattering. As this book goes to press, the January 6th Committee has taken a "summer recess" after completing their first eight hearings. I'm including a few reflecting on some of the key moments during Trump's (one, and for all our sakes I trust only) term in office – along with some more recent ones reflecting on his continuing, farcical, maddening, dangerous post-presidential behavior.

What If –
(March 21, 2018)

If you can keep your hair when all about you
Are losing theirs and blaming it on you,
If you can trust that Mike Flynn won't sell out you,
And make up facts with every day that's new;
If you can wait… oh, Jesus – who're we kidding?
You lie and yet insist we should believe;
If you can get Marc Short to do your bidding,
And watch as all your staffers start to leave:

If you can scream – but not scream at McMaster;
If you can think – and not make thoughts your aim;
If choice is only Carnage or Disaster,
The fault for which you'll never take the blame;
If you can bear to hear the truth from others,
Twisting knives already plunged in place,
Or watch as "Fox & Friends" chooses your druthers,
And stoop so low you barely can save face:

If you can make one heap of all your winnings
And risk it on another shaky bet,
And lose, and start again at your beginnings
And never breathe a word about your debt;

If you can force your heart and nerve and sinew
To keep reversing all your points of view,
And so hold on when Dems call bullshit on you,
Once more you'll tweet the comeback of: "FAKE NEWS!"

If you can talk with crowds about your virtue
While porn stars and nude models claim you touched;
If nothing Putin does seems to alert you;
Tax cuts for middle class, but not too much;
If you can drain the swamp this very hour
And keep your distance from Bob Mueller's reach,
You and your girth may hold on to your power,
And – which is more – you might not get impeached!

Sorry Seems to be the Hardest Word
(May 14, 2018)

A person who's an aide of mine joked John McCain was dying.
Most everyone who heard about it found it horrifying.
Some say that I should fire her, or send her on safari –
But that won't happen: Trump administration don't do "sorry."

We're trying to put a spin on it, and rail against the leak,
'Cause if we say, "We're sorry," then it makes us all look weak.
I've never made a statement that required a retraction,
So all those working for me now adopt the same reaction.

Some years ago I said I would apologize – if wrong.
I promise that I will, when that occasion comes along.
The worst thing I am guilty of might be hyperbole,
But expressions of regret? Not found in my philology.

The media comes after me, with laptops overheating,
Sometimes when all I'm guilty of is carelessly retweeting.

I'll never say I'm sorry for somebody else's words:
I can't be blamed when I am just repeating what I've heard.

The mainstream media keeps track of what they call my lies,
But not for anything I've said will I apologize.
The consequences likewise for this woman will be zero,
Since during the campaign I mocked McCain: "captured war hero."

Speaking your own truth: idea put forth by Oprah Winfrey.
I've always thought like that, and it's allowed me to live sin-free.
Not I, nor any on my staff, regret the things we've said.
McCain may have brain cancer, but it's my team that's brain dead.

Pardon Me?
(June 4, 2018)

I once made a statement of some notoriety, telling the world I could shoot
some schmuck in the middle of Fifth Avenue; voters still wouldn't give me the boot.
Now, thanks to my lawyer, I know who to aim for – I wouldn't just pick off some homie:
According to R. Giuliani, it seems I could legally murder James Comey.

I cannot be charged, irregardless of crimes I commit while I serve as the POTUS.
The cops could show up and run all through Miranda, but I wouldn't pay any notice.
They'd try to arrest me and take fingerprints while insisting, "We're here to accost – you must
come with in the squad car." But they couldn't touch me or claim I turned Comey to posthumous.

I see lots of chances to get away clean as the rule of law quickly relaxes:
collusion, obstruction, (this murder of course) and the best of all: "Hands off my taxes!"
I'm already handing out pardons like lollipops; stacked twenty-deep on my shelf.
But the one I'm most anxious to put into play is the one I will sign for myself.

All kinds of past geniuses – mostly the evil ones – scheme to pull off perfect crimes,
and thanks to the brilliance of all my attorneys, they've worked out a method where I'm
safe from being subpoenaed for anything I might have done (or will do) that is criminal.
Including if I am caught lying without meaning to, due to factors subliminal.

But really – I'd rather just feel free to roam 'round the city and bust up big fights
like Batman. I'd do it – except I'm not sure I'll be able to squeeze into tights.
One day I'd retire; pack up my belongings and spend all my days on the beach,
since Congress can't take steps to lock me up, even if all of them vote to impeach.

Big Man on Hippocampus

(September 28, 2018)

(Brett Kavanaugh)

I drink a lot of beer. I like beer. Beer is what I like to drink. But never once have brewskis compromised the way I act or think.

Now today I sit here, asked to justify some high school frolic:
There's no way my lifestyle then could be considered alcoholic.

Allegations made against me all are false; that's what I'm claiming.
Democrats, some left-wing groups, and – natch – the Clintons I am blaming.
To lay this all to rest for good: investigation's worth pursuing.
(Unless of course you mean the FBI, since they know what they're doing.)

Did I watch the testimony given here by my accuser?
No, I didn't; saw no need, since I deny I'm her abuser.
I will watch it later in a more relaxing atmosphere.
Quietly, where I can pay attention – while I drink more beer.

Democrats claim what I say is fabricated and conniving.
I won't cop to anything at all, except: I love imbibing.
Dr. Ford said caffeine helped her focus and maintain some leverage;
Glad that works for her. Myself – I much prefer an adult beverage.

My friend with a drinking problem wrote a book – a work of fiction.
If you mention it, you're making fun of some guy with addictions.
A roman à clef, it's said one character was based on my life.
Not remotely true: that guy drank Bud, and I drink Miller High Life.

Yes, I went to parties: we drank beer, and danced, and played Parcheesi.
Never did I drink 'til I blacked out, forgetting something sleazy.
Let's look at my calendar from '82 – all documented.
I list every single time I chugged down beverages fermented.

During my remarks, there's several times when I became
unhinged.
One of them when Klobuchar opined my drinking might be
"binge."
Sure, sometimes I vomited – but that's due to my weak intestine.
No way I had anything to do with that night now in question.

I was out of town for every summer weekend… so I'm thinking
There's no way that I was at a party filled with sex and drinking.
Certainly what happened to Ms. Ford made for a very bleak day.
No way that I could have been involved – unless it was a
weekday.

Trying to save my chance at the Supreme Court, I did something
drastic:
Let my freak flag fly with no restraint and went full-on
bombastic.
As the next day's sun arose, it seems I made the proper choice –
Rants and raves and indignation overwhelmed a victim's voice.

Bul-let Us Pray
(October 27, 2018)

Not sure why people are agog
that I said, "Guns in synagogue."
You'd be safer in a church
with a sniper in the lurch.
Monks who call themselves a Buddhist
must now arm in case of shootist.
Feel safer in the sanctuary:
Open carry; be less wary.
Ammunition clips to load a
Sig Sauer pistol in pagoda.
In gurdwara, every Sikh
is taught the proper gun technique.

Arsenal for the Bahá'í
to tell some lousy punk, "BUH-bye!"

Gunman interrupts a Mass?
Pop a cap right in his ass.
Interloper when you baptize?
Aim right in between that chap's eyes.
Midst of something eucharistic?
Time for you to go ballistic.

We need to have more trigger squeezes
so Christians can stay tight with Jesus.
Jewish people: don't abhor a
rifle to protect your Torah.
Allah says you'll stay alive
if you bring along a .45.
Protect most all religious factions
with Winchester's lever action.

Church guards must be armed today
to keep the flock out of harm's way.
If you are an atheist,
better hope that zealot missed.
Time to join the NRA
if you want to calmly pray.
God now teaches us a lesson:
Father, Son, and Smith & Wesson.

War Zeroes
(November 19, 2018)

If I had been a Navy Seal
I would have been the real deal.

Unlike Bill Clinton – take my shot and
then claim: now bin Laden gotten.

If I had been in Delta Force,
I'd save the day again, of course.
I'd tell Somalis, "You will wish you
never fought in Mogadishu."

If I had been a Green Beret,
I'd chase the Vietcong away.
I'd be the first one they'd send in
to overthrow that Hồ Chí Minh.

If I'd been in the Secret Service,
I'd have made Lee Harvey nervous.
That magic bullet's strange trajectory
would slow and stop once it came next to me.

If I had been an Army Ranger,
I'd keep the U.S. out of danger.
I'd tell my Mom and Poppa, "See ya'!"
And then go liberate Korea.

If I had been at Lincoln's side,
I'd stop John Wilkes Booth in one stride.
I'd keenly pick up on his temper;
no *tyrannis* or *sic semper*.

If I had been a S.W.A.T. team leader,
I'd take out those bottom feeders.
Save line dancers and school children
before some bad guy got to kill one.

Into grave danger I would step in,
even not armed with a weapon.

Hand-to-hand, or tossing Tic-Tacs,
or confuse them with my syntax.

But when time came for me to do it,
due to bone spurs I said, "Screw it!"
The closest that I've come to combat:
those true war heroes I lob bombs at.

No Guts, No Glory
(November 29, 2018)

My gut tells me more than your brain ever could – and you know that my gut is immense.
I'd much rather do what my gut tells me to than be briefed one more time by Mike Pence.
I go with my gut and decide in the moment; don't like to prepare in advance.
I hope you're impressed what I'm using for brains is now bursting right out of my pants.

You know I'm a genius – I heard someone say it (you caught me: I'm quoting myself).
My staff hands me binders; they're chock full of data – I put them right back on the shelf.
I don't need to read and I don't need to study. I walk in a room and I just know
exactly what needs to be done, who should do it, and how to attack it with gusto.

I know more about the economy; more than the Chair of the Fed seems to know.
I'm not at all happy with what he is doing – perhaps it is time he should go.

I dumped an advisor when he opposed tariffs and then brought in Kudlow, a pundit.
He goes on TV and he advocates free trade, but can't explain how we will fund it.

I've got the highest IQ you can have, since it's based on the size of my waist.
Tillerson called me a moron (an "effing" one) – I quickly had him replaced.
Using my gut as the source of all knowledge means I'll carry on as a glutton.
You've got less brains in your head, as a rule, than you'll find wedged in my belly button.

I know the best words and went to the best schools and my memory is just super.
Don't be surprised that my think tank's a toilet – and I am the Number One Pooper.
I'm even smarter than those I appoint who attended an Ivy League college.
I'll eat those Ivies for breakfast and then spend the next hour crapping out knowledge.

No one is smarter than me (or than I). Anyway – you don't need me to tell this.
Not only smart, but so handsome! In younger days, they say I looked just like Elvis.
I know the most about NATO and trade, infrastructure and…
Do you know what?
You'll find less smarts in a room full of Einsteins than I've got lodged here in my gut.

Sob Stories
(April 10, 2019)

I am the victim of a coup.
My taxes I won't show to you.
My A.G. thinks there was some spying.
Michael Cohen keeps on lying.
My health care plan is wait-and-see.
My latest motto: "Woe is me."

For reasons of which I'm unwitting,
My employees keep on quitting.
Secretaries are all "Acting."
Barr is busy with redacting.
Rallies now a place for swearing.
Grievances – relentless airing.

Correspondents' dinner – skipping.
GDP shows signs of slipping.
Dad was born in… Germany?
Immigrants are vermin. We
Must build a wall to keep us safe.
The Constitution makes me chafe.

Biden's problem: likes to smooch,
But I skate scot-free grabbing cooch.
Claim I'm best at nearly all things,
Yet I have to cheat at golfing.
Merkel makes me quite uneasy;
Know who I think's great? el-Sisi.

A walking contradiction, I
Who spurns truth over fiction; why?
I state I am this country's savior;
Disregard my strange behavior.

And yet, these storms I'm sure to weather
Until Dems get their shit together.

On a Scale of One to Contentious
(May 2, 2019)

Bill Barr did a fantastic job, he's quite the legal genius.
So tightly we're aligned, you can't slide dental floss between us.
He sat before the Senate; his defense of me audacious –
even if his grasp of right and wrong appears fallacious.

Investigation thought by me unfair means I can end it;
a position so absurd that even I can't comprehend it.
If I'm accused of doing something wrong, yet don't agree,
I get to say the rule of law does not apply to me.

He said to force an underling to lie was nothing criminal,
and actions that I took were not overt; instead, subliminal.
He helped explain that "flipping" means, to me, the same as "lying."
So "please don't flip" means "tell the truth" – that's all I was implying.

Bill Barr said he was grappling with "suggest" – a tricky word.
When offered some alternatives, like "hinted" and "inferred,"
he still chose not to offer any answer found definitive –
then got right back on track and picked up splitting his infinitives.

The memo he released outlined the principal conclusions,
but don't call it a "summary" – that led to some confusion.
When Mueller got in contact and expressed dissatisfaction,
Barr told him, "You made work for me by skipping the redactions."

The tension in the room got turned up several notches higher
when Hirono had her turn; called me a grifter and a liar
and said Barr had sacrificed his once-thought-decent reputation
by abandoning his principles through our association.

Regarding this report, Barr sometimes got a little hyper.
It may have been his baby, but he wouldn't check the diaper.
The underlying evidence he did not look at – strange. It
was analogous to smelling poop and saying, "Here – you change
it."

But all in all, I felt the job that Barr did was fantastic,
since his approach to truth is just like mine – which is "elastic."
Now Dems want Bill Barr to resign; that argument's not fecund.
My first word to them starts with "F" – and "y-o-u" comes
second.

Me-Day
(June 5, 2019)

I was never a fan of the Vietnam War. If I had been, I would
have enlisted.
If I'd gotten my hands around Hồ Chí Minh's neck, I'd have
taken him out – unassisted.
Unfortunately, it was not meant to be; I had medical problems
and such.
If I could fight Nazis, I'd give it a shot. But the Viet Cong? Eh,
not so much.

If the Vietnam War had been closer, perhaps, with objectives not
quite so oblique, then
I might have signed up and gone over to serve – if they'd let me
come home on the weekends.

A terrible war that was far, far away; in a country nobody had heard of.
Not a fan – I'd have cut our involvement in half, or perhaps even down to a third of.

I wasn't out marching or carrying placards; I was not one who had demanded a
Quick end to the war, but please give me some credit: at least I did not move to Canada.
Instead of enlisting, I got those deferments; some student, and one that was medical.
Believe me – in combat I would have been deadly. Of course, that is all hypothetical.

I would not have minded at all to have served. But, regretfully, I didn't get to.
I graciously let someone else take my place. That is one poor schmuck I owe a debt to.
But now I'm rebuilding our forces at levels that I think is going to make up for it.
I already know all the lyrics to Reveille. Therefore, no need to wake up for it.

Life would be different if I had been born in the Twenties; that decade was Roaring.
I could have stormed onto Omaha Beach – whereas Battle of Huế? Kinda boring.
I'm looking forward to honoring soldiers on D-Day. It's quite an occasion.
They fought for freedom and justice – and I fought as well: to secure draft evasion.

Prodding the Squad
(July 15, 2019)

Go back to where you came from – which in my case is Jamaica
(that's the neighborhood in Queens where I was born, in New
York City).
All my enemies now think I used a tweet so I could make a
racist statement about four progressive women – what a pity.

I was only trying to make the point our country is the greatest;
those who criticize our government with words both loud and
vicious
should be handed travel vouchers, by next Tuesday at the latest,
to return to their home shitholes. Or, at least, that's what my
wish is.

There is absolutely nothing that is racist in me saying
that they use disgusting language, yet they call themselves
"progressive"
while the countries they descend from all appear to be decaying.
I am speaking simple truths and don't know why that's found
aggressive.
Just because I used some phrasing in a manner that's suggestive
that these women don't belong here doesn't mean that I abhor
them –
some traditions in their native lands can even be thought festive!
I'm just saying that they're Commies, and Pelosi should ignore
them.

If you criticize our country, you are always free to leave it.
You can get a U.S. passport or a driver's license, but no
one who truly loves this land should call me "racist" – don't
believe it.
It is not a sign of prejudice to call a spade a… uh-oh.

Why would I pick on these women? Well, it shouldn't be a mystery:
to distract from all my failures, and avoid the glare of bright sun.
I've made many statements like this, if you just look at my history:
keeping folks of color out ensures our nation is a white one.

Wretched Refusal
(August 13, 2019)

If you're hungry, we won't feed you.
And for God's sake – don't be poor.
Hope that plaque did not mislead you:
you're not welcome anymore.

Can you stand on both your own feet
and not crush our country's toes?
Do not ask us for a loan, Pete;
we will not be granting those.

If you're likely to use food stamps,
or you lack toothbrush and comb,
You will doubtlessly be screwed, Gramps –
turn around and go back home.

Sure, we used to take the tired;
masses yearning for a breath –
but, unless you can get hired,
that's an ancient shibboleth.

With a lamp that now burns clean coal,
we've raised registration fees.
Entry now a Byzantine goal:
try some other nation, please.

Shooting My Mouth Off
(August 21, 2019)

The issue isn't gun control: we have a mental problem.
As fast as Democrats come up with fixes, I will lob them
back into their laps while claiming that their slope is getting slippery.
Universal background checks are nothing more than frippery.

Right after the El Paso shooting, and the one in Dayton,
I said that something must be done right now – we're tired of waitin'.
But as the weeks go by, it's clear I never really meant it.
More bloodshed sure to come; I'll have done nothing to prevent it.

A person pulls the trigger; trigger's not pulled by the gun.
A weapon slumbers innocent – until used by someone.
Until it's locked and loaded, every firearm merely lingers.
The problem's not the ammo; it's the guy with itchy fingers.

The issue isn't guns in hands – it's who can get their hands on
something that our Number 2 Amendment says this country stands on.
And when even Lindsey Graham says a semi-automatic
is essential, you can see why gun control is problematic.

No, the problem here is people who are vexed with mental illness.
There's no way we'll all be safe from outbursts murderous until this
diagnosis can be made for every nut job in existence.
(How ironic even "red flag" laws are now meeting resistance.)

Forced to choose between a forward step or none – I'll choose the latter,
and fall back on thoughts and prayers the next time people have to scatter.
I'll claim Democrats will take your guns and make you do without them.
But mass shootings? It's clear I won't do a goddam thing about them.

Elements of a Perfect Phone Call
(October 7, 2019)

To make a perfect phone call: first, you dial the country code.
Next, offer admiration for a victory bestowed.
Remind the other person of the debt that you are owed,
Then intimate a favor (so you won't be quid pro quo'd).

Be careful with your language, and a little bit obtuse,
to guard against rogue listeners whose lips, perhaps, are loose.
Don't spell out what you're asking for; just let your friend deduce.
Your words, if they are twisted, could be fashioned as a noose.

I'll offer one suggestion: you had best stay off the speaker.
You never know who in the room may prove to be a leaker.
When Rudy Giuliani is your personal truth-seeker,
be careful: his defense may make your prospects look much bleaker.

The thing that you must guard against is one who blows the whistle;
the law sure makes it difficult to mandate their dismissal.
This really isn't treason, but it's certain you will bristle
if it leads to your impeachment — which the polls suggest that this'll.

Id Pro Quo
(January 14, 2020)

It doesn't really matter what I do or why I do it;
doesn't matter what the reasons are, or whether I thought through it.
I don't have to seek approval or ask anyone's permission:
I'm your President, and that means I'm correct – by definition.

The ends will always justify the means, so what's the problem?
If some bombs resolve an issue, then just go ahead and lob 'em.
If a drone strike isn't authorized, it really doesn't matter.
If a woman dares to criticize, just tweet some insults at her.

If you want to build a wall, but hit a snag with its approval,
raid the military budget to secure the funds' removal.
If the Constitution says that what you're doing is baloney,
just dismiss our founding fathers and proclaim a section "phony."

When you're caught up in a lie, despite your innocence-proclaiming,
point a finger at your rival and accuse them of the same thing.
When the facts do not add up, or undermine what you're asserting,
then create your own statistics, even if they're disconcerting.

If a foreign leader treats his horde in ways that make your gut weak,
just ignore it – if he plants his lips upon your ample butt cheek.
If a family seeking freedom flees here for their own survival:
send them back; have them arrested; split them up upon arrival.

If you rail about due process, but the evidence indicts you;
if free speech – not yours, but others' – only angers and incites you;

if you're not a man of scruples but an easily coerced one:
then perhaps you can be President. So what if you're the worst one?

Don't You Know It
(February 4, 2020)

I know that when my hair needs styling, I don't use a barber.
I know that something happened (not sure what) in Pearl Harbor.
I know that Mayor Pete looks like he's saying, "What, me worry?"
But I didn't know the Kansas City Chiefs play in Missouri.

I know that call I made regarding Ukraine aid: perfecto.
I know my power as the President must go unchecked, so
I claim the Constitution gives authority unfettered.
Though that's not true – Republicans to my hip now are tethered.

I know you flush ten times to get a doody down the toilet.
I know the ending to that "Fight Club" movie, but won't spoil it.
I know that my inauguration crowd: the biggest all-time.
I know I'll be acquitted of some large, and several small, crimes.

I know when you're a star that you can grab chicks by the lady parts.
I know in England when somebody "trumps" – you are afraid he farts.
I know that a concussion is not much more than a headache.
I know there's truth in media reports each time I've said, "FAKE."

I know more about ISIS than the generals all claim to.
I know I'll never own up to mistakes; instead, I'll blame you.

I know I'd rather lie than tell a truth that doesn't suit me.
I know I've let Vlad Putin and Kim Jong-un both delude me.

I know I've sidestepped actions that the Dems all thought impeachable.
I know I won't be censured, since I'm now all but unreachable.
I know if I'm allowed to get away with all my misdeeds,
then clearly we are on the road to hell – that's where all this leads.

Kiss My Aspirations Goodbye
(March 13, 2020)

I don't want people dying. That's what I'm all about.
I'm thoroughly against death – of this, there should be no doubt.
So if coronavirus should result in more demises, we
are sure to see me ream out some poor schmuck who now advises me.

I keep assuring people there's no barrier to testing.
(That's a fact all health professionals are currently contesting.)
People now ask if the ventilators on hand are sufficient;
let me answer with another question: What am I – omniscient?

Should I declare a national emergency? I seem a-
-fraid to take this step, which quickly would free up more funds for FEMA.
I have memorized the Stafford Act, with all the powers it grants me:
in front of me are trees, and yet the forest it seems I can't see.

Nearly every step I've taken has received dismissive thumbs-down.
And now, every single day, another public figure comes down

with the virus – some are even pictured right next to my shoulder,
yet I won't get tested (risk is in the eye of the beholder).

Dr. Fauci is the expert, and he says things will get better
(sometime after they get worse); it seems I underplay the threat. Sure,
the economy is tanking; I seem clueless. But what's nice is
odds are good that my administration won't outlive this crisis.

I Am the Very Muddle
(April 6, 2020)

(with apologies to Gilbert and/or Sullivan)

I don't have fullest confidence in this inspector general.
Support for my appointees is both fleeting and ephemeral.
The circumstances leading to his sacking – not amenable.
But I found his behavior to be flippant and untenable.
His action with the whistleblower I have found lamentable,
and therefore Michael Atkinson I now declare expendable.
About my perfect Ukraine call I surely made a lot o' news,
with alternative facts about the transcript offered to confuse.

[CHORUS]
With alternative facts about the transcript offered to confuse
With alternative facts about the transcript offered to confuse
With alternative facts about the transcript offered to con-rootin'-fuse

I will not wear a mask to ward off sneezing or a hacking cough.
The whistleblower was a fake and someone should sue his ass off.
In short, in matters economic, military, medical –
I am the very model of positions found heretical.

[CHORUS]
In short, in matters economic, military, medical –
He is the very model of positions found heretical

If someone has coronavirus, I think it's OK they choose
to take the drugs that I promote, and disregard what the Fake News
is saying about chloroquine and how it isn't proven yet.
So, take it or don't take it – either way, I won't get too upset.
Our program to protect small business payroll rolled out perfectly.
I had a captain fired who bitched; removed him from the bright blue sea.
The insights of key experts it is clear that I am keen without.
Each passing day it's clearer of control I am careening out.

[CHORUS]
Each passing day it's clearer of control he is careening out
Each passing day it's clearer of control he is careening out
Each passing day it's clearer of control he is careen-areen-ing out

When I can have a bill passed, which is worth more than two-trillion bucks.
When I close all our borders to cut back on foreigners' influx.
When anyone who's not a family member I'm more wary at.
And as the bodies stack up, we're not sure where they'll be buried at.
When my Attorney General suspends the corpus habeas.
When I say China had the most afflicted, though it may be us.
In short (just like my fingers), it appears I have no strategy.
Some say my disapproval rating's not yet reached its apogee.

[CHORUS]
Some say his disapproval rating's not yet reached its apogee
Some say his disapproval rating's not yet reached its apogee
Some say his disapproval rating's not yet reached its apo-crapo-gee

Will we survive to see another decade in this century?
I think you will admit my term has been quite an adventure, we
will see if voters back me up, or if they've become hesitant –
increasing odds Joe Biden will take over as your President.

[CHORUS]
We'll see if voters back him up, or if they've become hesitant –
since we need someone competent to serve as our next President.

Son of a Bleach
(April 24, 2020)

You know I'm not a doctor – but of course I could have been,
that's why, up until a week ago, I touted chloroquine.
Now, new evidence suggests that might have been an overreach,
so instead I'll tout another treatment: shooting up with bleach.

Nearly everybody's got a jug of Clorox in their homes,
so this treatment wouldn't cost a dime to fix your chromosomes.
It's another brilliant plan of mine to give all folks protection
from this malady, by means of self-administered injection.

For some of you, the use of needles may prove to be tough. It
would be fine, then, to pull out a can of Lysol and just huff it.
Maybe gargle with some bleach, or add it to your morning beverage –
and the only risk, besides the taste, is suffering a hemorrhage.

I also think that UV light is showing some potential,
so I'll make a proclamation – bona fide and presidential –
telling everyone to go outside for more than just a minute
and let sunlight cascade on your bod and kill whatever's in it.

I'm just here to give ideas and to offer up suggestions,
then to lay into reporters who have dared to ask me questions.
The response to what I'm advocating? Every doctor cringed.
With each passing day, it's clear I have completely come
unhinged.

Better to Remain Silent
(June 6, 2020)

(Just to refresh your memory: Trump invoked George Floyd's name ten days after his death at the hands of the police, while reviewing a stronger-than-expected monthly jobs report.)

If George is looking down on us, I hope that he would say
there's great things again now happening here in the USA.
I believe, from his perspective, he's receiving great enjoyment
as he witnesses how wrong all were regarding May's employment.

It's a great day here for everyone, and also him – at least, when
he became aware arrests were made of all four rogue policemen.
I'll bet there are a lot of thoughts now running through his head;
there's so much to celebrate, and take his mind off being dead.

Today's the greatest comeback in the history of our nation
(well, "come back" is not the phrase to use in George's situation).
Some awful unemployment numbers seems we have avoided.
Gee, if only others had the same perspective that George Floyd
did.

Although no longer with us, I feel moved now by his spirit.
If he whispers in my ear, I'd swear that I can almost hear it.
He might offer words of wisdom, and for me he'd offer praise.
He'd know all about tear gasses; not the same as pepper sprays.

Peaceful protestors and looters – he's aware there's no comparison.
A shame he's gone, since now he's my top African-American.
It's a great day for equality – but, all things being equal,
all the promises I'm making to minorities are treacle.

I've compared myself to Lincoln, who proclaimed emancipation.
LBJ passed several bills that were a cause for celebration.
Who abolished segregation in the service? That was Harry.
My approach to those who struggle – best described as…
fragmentary.

To invoke the name of George Floyd was another act of violence.
Cruel to put words in his mouth when, for all time, his voice is silenced.
But I couldn't help myself, because my ego was engorged
over furloughed workers coming back – and so I uttered, "George."

Other words that spilled from my lips: "weak," "control," and "dominate."
I've done nothing to soothe outrage, but instead keep spewing hate.
When it comes to race relations, it's quite clear I have my limits.
So don't hold your breath for change, or – worse – stop breathing for nine minutes.

Stop Picking on Me
(June 30, 2020)

I don't pay attention to my daily briefing;
I have a short span of attention.
Through a copy of Penthouse I'd rather be leafing
so, sometimes, I miss a key mention.
I gloss over things that I should find compelling (we
ought to make bullet points bolder),
so I didn't realize someone was telling me:
Russia's been killing our soldiers.

When this hit the papers and people first learned,
my response was, of course, quite defensive.
Instead of appalled, I appeared unconcerned:
didn't find Russia's conduct offensive.
Some top GOPers were briefed before I was;
I'm still in the dark, I am claiming.
The question on everyone's mind now is: why does
our POTUS side-step Putin-shaming?

My press person says there's opinions dissenting,
and that's why nobody had told me.
I'll latch onto that, in the hope circumventing
the truth means no scandal enfolds me.
I want to bring Russia back to the G8
which, in light of this news, sure seems heinous.
The comeback I've offered may not resonate:
I'm a top-notch, Class A ignoramus.

Brain He Lacks
(July 23, 2020)

I'm cognitively there, as regards mental acuity.
Test results I'm glad to share: I'm replete with ingenuity.

I took a special test and exceeded expectations;
doctors said, "Your score's the best out of all examinations!"

They read five words from a list, then they asked me to repeat them;
also said, "Sir, we insist – there's no need for you to tweet them."
Then, once thirty minutes passed, they confirmed my recollection.
My performance: unsurpassed; my score: unheard-of perfection.

This proves my brain is the best out of all brains they've inspected.
Everyone should be impressed; I outpaced what was expected.
While I struggle with my weight and I keep on getting fatter,
about this there's no debate: can't find fault with my gray matter.

When compared to other Presidents, no other was as brainy
(of course, I'm the one who says it). Went ballistic on Liz Cheney
when I heard of her disdain at things she doesn't care one whit for.
So I think, as far as brains, it's clear Liz Cheney has got shit for.

Now we'll wait and see if Joe, who I say is just a brick shy
of a thorough mental load, takes the test and does as slick. I
have proclaimed my strong belief that his cognition is diminished;
but I didn't think this through – since if he passes, I am finished.

Scrambled Egghead
(August 7, 2020)

Intelligence is beautiful, it's basic and it's pure.
So when it comes to voting and ensuring it's secure,
I'll draw upon my genius and I'll use my common sense
to claim that mail-in voting has a fraud risk that's immense.

There's a difference between mail-in and what I call absentee,
or at least that's what *I* say – but now, in actuality,
they are pretty much the same thing, which most states have
implemented.
Any fraud's all but unheard of; seems it's something I've
invented.

My intelligence is also what I've called upon when I
say that children are immune from COVID-19. So then – why
are there now several hundred thousand children who've been
diagnosed?
That's a trivial percentage, from my observation post.

I'm a very stable genius; I'm the smartest of the smart –
yet I seem to get befuddled when I show someone a chart
using figures that are cherry-picked and on the whole invalid,
and when challenged on the facts can only come back with word
salad.

I like to make broad statements, with positions absolute:
The facts are not in evidence; conclusions in dispute.
I'll offer these remarks despite how far from truth they stray,
and put my true sagacity on national display.

He's Mailing It In Now
(September 3, 2020)

I'll set the record for votes cast
in hopes I'll finish first, not last.
If one vote's good, then two are better;
ignore the spirit and the letter
of the laws regarding voting.
Here's the latest scheme I'm floating:
Vote by mail, and then again
in-person; see what happens when

you try to vote another time.
(Some say that constitutes a crime.)
They tabulate your mail-in vote?
The chance of fraud might be remote.
They let you cast a second ballot?
Leaves a sour taste on my palate.
I've counseled that's what you should do
(perhaps I didn't think this through);
to vote twice is a felony:
at polls, on top of absentee.
And while the risk is miniscule,
I'm trying to make the case that you'll
be cheated on Election Day
if Dems – as I suspect – just may
send unsought ballots through the mail.
I'll claim fraud on a massive scale;
some folks don't want to exercise
their constitutional franchise.
Instead, they'll choose to sit this out –
their ballots we can do without;
a plebiscite dumped in their lap.
Encourage votes? I sense a trap.
A rigged election: it could lurk
if votes crawl out of the woodwork.
I've got the backing of Bill Barr –
who's unsure what each state's laws are.
Elective pandemonium:
please vote – don't stop at only one.

Deduction Reasoning
(September 28, 2020)

I have said avoiding taxes is just proof that I am smart,
and reducing liability's not science, but an art.

So, among the most creative of allowances, I dare say,
were the tens of thousands I wrote off for all those cans of
hairspray.

An audit meant at my returns you couldn't take a peek. It
was the flimsiest excuse for keeping all that data secret.
Richard Nixon, in the midst of Watergate, released his taxes –
but not me. It was the failing New York Times who first
unpacked this.

I paid not one cent of income tax in ten of fifteen years,
and for two of those – just seven-hundred fifty it appears.
I filed a massive refund that might not have been legitimate,
but despite the shaky dodge it rests upon, I still submitted it.

I own a huge estate: it's not a home, but an investment.
I've refused to share my filings in response to each request sent.
I paid several hundred thousands when Ivanka was consulted
on a hotel deal, and made use of the credit that resulted.

An image of abundant wealth's what fueled my rise to power;
I lose money on most everything I own, except Trump Tower.
I bleed money at my golf courses; unloaded stocks I held.
My abuse of our tax system is perhaps unparalleled.

I've dismissed the *Times'* reporting, claiming (no surprise) FAKE
NEWS;
said the I.R.S. is most unfair, for years I've been abused.
My supporters won't abandon me – they all know who I am,
but the way that I've portrayed myself is nothing but a sham.

Relapse in Judgment
(October 13, 2020)

My doctor says I pose no risk of transmission;
for several days I have now been fever-free.
So much for this COVID-19 imposition;
I'm back to insisting there's vote thievery.

I'll kiss all the guys and the beautiful women
(but no need to worry – I'll smooch with no tongue).
With bluff and bravado I'm once again brimmin'
in front of the large mask-less crowds I'm among.

When you are the Prez, can't be locked in a basement;
you've got to get out and take risks time to time.
But now I'm immune and without self-effacement.
My ego's inflated; my pump's again primed.

I learned quite a bit from the illness I went through,
yet even while frail, I displayed showmanship. A
miraculous comeback by your President. You
won't learn the specifics, since I've invoked HIPAA.

I'm back out campaigning and sharing my knowledge,
repeating my claims that this plague's disappearing.
I've got the support of some whites with a college
degree; it's the loss of blue-collar I'm fearing.

There's three weeks to go and I'm back at full stamina.
(Some are concerned there's a chance that I'll relapse.)
Yet I claim it's Biden that should be examined, a
ridiculous slander. What's Joe's response? He laughed.

The polls suggest I am no longer the favorite,
but I won't accept that, despite what some murmur.
My time in the White House? Perhaps I should savor it –
since odds are increasing I'll be a one-termer.

Transitioning Bender
(November 21, 2020)

I refuse to give in;
I keep saying I won.
In the world of has-beens
I'll soon be Number One.

I will battle in court
with a crack legal team –
who appear a brick short;
of the crop, they're not cream.

I'll exert undue pressure
and urge retribution.
I need a refresher
on our Constitution.

Joe won? I'll ignore him
and trash him on Twitter.
All hope for decorum's
gone right down the shitter.

Can't tell fact from fiction,
and I seem perplexed here.
My childish conniption
will go into next year.

I plan to go out
with a bang, not a whimper.

You miss times, no doubt,
when transitions were simpler.

Distressed Address
(December 3, 2020)

This may be the most important speech I've ever made:
a chance to share conspiracies, and also throw some shade.
We used to have elections in a day; not anymore,
so let me share thoughts – none of which you'd give a penny for.

I have no higher duty than defending all our laws –
except when they apply to me (please stifle your guffaws).
We must support elections that are free and also fair.
(That's only if I won – a loss means fraud I will declare.)

Three-quarters of an hour was the length of time I bellowed.
It's clear that, since Election Day, not one whit have I mellowed.
I shared countless conspiracies, all which have been disproven,
but I'll latch on to any scheme if it keeps me from losin'.

I led the charge of GOP success – so it's statistically
impossible that I could lose, I stated narcissistically.
The words I'm saying now will be disparaged and demeaned,
but worth one final shot before electors are convened.
I've made it clear I feel this was a national disgrace.
I spoke with an expression of disgust upon my face.
A speech filled with absurdities, but here's what's most absurd:
a record day for Covid deaths – yet I said not a word.

An enemy, I labelled Raffensperger, of the people,
while over many people's eyes I'm trying to pull sheep's wool.
As I make these unfounded claims, you really should be wary –
since truths contained within there's not a single solitary.

A Riotous Success
(January 12, 2021)

The moment called for reconciliation and some healing;
that onslaught I belatedly called "heinous."
The riot I incited with my calls to stop the stealing?
I governed with my head right up my anus.

Our tempers must be cooled and we must have some calm restored.
(I said those words but really didn't mean them.
Appearing impotent's a look that I could ill-afford
with my flock once I tweeted to convene them.)

My only goal: ensuring the integrity of votes,
with confidence and faith placed in the outcome.
Let's all ignore the violence my attitude promotes;
no need for panic – is there any doubt? Some...

They've analyzed my speech, my words – they all thought to a "T"
all statements that I've offered were appropriate.
Although some in the GOP are now upset with me,
most act as though I've given them an opiate.

To all of my supporters: you are wonderful, and yet
I know you're disappointed, but keep fighting.
Our journey's just beginning, so there's no need for regret.
The *next* rebellion: even more exciting.

(At this point, I took a break from Trump-themed poetry for about a year... and then he drew me back in.)

Vlad All Over
(February 24, 2022)

While the rest of the world seems appalled about Vlad
and his steps toward a war – I, for one, am quite glad.
I believe that my dear Russian comrade's a "genius."
It's clear I believe there's still ardor between us.

In the choice between freedom – or none – in Ukraine,
I support savvy Vladimir Putin, whose brain
is quite nearly the equal of mine, folks, and hence
I embrace him with zeal (but, no longer, Mike Pence).

Putin says at least two parts of Ukraine are sovereign,
so he plans to send in a peacekeeping squadron,
like <u>we</u> should commence at our southernmost border.
I'm clearly aroused by this brand-new world order.

I know Putin quite well; in fact – very, very.
He's long been my friend. *Biden's* my adversary.
Some say I'm deranged – what the hell do they know?
Know who else praises Vlad? Now-slim Mike Pompeo.

Have you heard of my new internet apparatus?
I call it "Truth Social" (its rollout: disastrous).
It's gonna be better than Twitter – purportedly.
(That's good – since it's now the sole outlet afforded me).

I make these pronouncements the world finds are shocking,
while Joe Biden's manhood I'll keep right on mocking,
and give my ascent to this tyrant so vile –
all to stay on the front page, and boost my profile.

It's clear I intend to return to the White House
(although *sans* Melania – my now out-of-sight spouse).

That rebound will be a most splendid occasion
(assuming I skate on alleged tax evasion).

I throw my support behind candidates who'll,
when compared to incumbents, appear to be fools.
And yet my endorsement they gladly accept
(that's because, to a person, they're dim and inept).

It's just one more sign of the breadth of my ego
to hold up a potentate as *mi amigo*.
Democracy? Feh… as a concept, it's done –
and that's why I keep on proclaiming I won.

Bunker Mentality
(March 30, 2022)

Many folks are asking, so I thought I would announce:
I made a hole-in-one! Rolled in behind the second bounce.
My shot was quite magnificent, which I proclaimed with hubris:
the witnesses were other men; all four of them were boob-less.

I struck it with a 5-iron that I pulled out of my bag.
My swing was better than the pros I played with (humblebrag).
This happened at a course I own, the one in West Palm Beach.
(You all remember who I am – the POTUS twice-impeached).

I mentioned in my statement that I don't like folks who brag, but
all my partners were impressed I had no need to make a lag putt.
Ernie Els has won 4 majors and he saw the ball go clank.
(My call log displays some gaps, just like Dick Nixon's tapes were blank.)

My golf game, I say humbly, is superior to most.
I just was called a "partner" by a Russian TV host.

In golf – and, frankly, everything – I'm known as a fast learner.
(Just one thing I'm not hip to: it's those prepaid phones called
"burner.")

According to some polls, my popularity is slidin',
so that's why I asked Putin to share dirt on Hunter Biden.
While everyone's obsessed with all the fighting in Ukraine,
I share news of my golf game (and employ legerdemain).

In golf, as in elections, final counts I'm known to fudge.
Such actions likely are corrupt, or so just said a judge.
Once struck, where golf balls end up is referred to as their "lie" –
and that's a term with which no one is more well-versed than I.

Overdue Rant
(June 19, 2022)

I DEMAND EQUAL TIME!!! I've got plenty to say.
One more sham Dem disgrace: same witch hunt, different day.
From an Unselect group; a committee that's Pseudo;
afraid of the truths about which I and you know.

A simple protest that just got out of hand,
as I tried to usurp every law of the land
to negate the results and extend my regime.
More were there than when MLK said, "I've a dream."

I do not accept blame for that Capitol surge;
'twas the fault of Mike Pence, who was lacking in courage.
And besides – hardly any of those in the throng
issued threats, brandished guns, or did anything wrong.

We have now heard three days of intense testifying
from those close to me – every one of them's lying.

I called Pence a "wimp," or so one guy said he heard
(I've not yet denied calling Mike Pence the p-word).

Witnesses threatened, in some cases ruined,
all just because they offered proof of a coup. And
by government servants we've now been betrayed.
(If you donated money to me – you've been played.)

This Committee, comprised of left-wingers and RINOs,
is all smoke and mirrors, as both you and I know.
I put out a statement – 12 single-spaced pages –
and carefully footnoted all of my rages.

Written during the throes of a Diet Coke binge,
this philippic is proof that I'm clearly unhinged.
I rehash every claim that's been thrown out of court,
overblown, or disproved. (Also – fuck you, Marc Short.)

I have claimed that Ivanka came close to a perjure
(I now regret backing the Trump-Kushner merger).
Having thrown my own flesh and blood under the bus
makes it clear my behavior is what's treasonous.

Unbottled Rage
(July 2, 2022)

My favorite food is ketchup; I will pour it on my steak:
my desire for this red condiment is one I cannot slake.
On Thanksgiving, I will slather it upon my Butterball –
and I even placed some ketchup on the Oval Office wall.

I was angry at that moment – like a raging, roiling sea –
having heard Bill Barr renounce his feckless loyalty to me.
What's the reason anyone would care about this sauce-y tidbit?
It provided quite an insight as to where my ire and id sit.

Now, the context for unearthing this unseemly revelation
was as part of an attempt to learn the risk I'd placed our nation
at by stubbornly insisting the election had been purloined;
my persistence ever-tougher, like a far-too-well-done sirloin.

It's alleged I knew that weapons were by some folks being toted
at the rally staged to claim that those who'd fraudulently voted
in the previous election shouldn't have their ballots counted.
(An attempted siege of Congress this mob subsequently
mounted.)

The young woman who provided this alarming testimony
was denounced by me quite loudly as a fake, bad news, a phony.
While I claimed I barely knew her, and refuted her assessment,
just a few stans backed me up – and now I'm wondering where
the rest went?

I'll deny, deny, deny – akin to Michael Flynn's strange answer
of the Fifth, the Fifth, the Fifth regarding power's peaceful
transfer.
Now there's rumors I am rushing to declare my latest bid:
it's a straight line to my ego from my wild, impulsive id.

Marital Blitz

As this book goes to press, my wife Carol and I have been married for over 41 years. After reading this section, please resist the urge to friend her on Facebook to ask, "WHY??"

Speaker of the House
(October 12, 2015)

Cruising through one of the big warehouse stores while waiting for the missus to decide on a pair of glasses, I spied a wireless TV soundbar on markdown. "I've got to have that," I convinced myself. I had a $10 gift card burning a hole in my wallet, making it an even more appealing deal, so when we walked out of the store my wife held a receipt for the promise of her new glasses in three weeks while I had a brand new toy to play with that very afternoon. I won.

Until I got home and unpacked my purchase. I'm not sure how "wireless" made it into the product description since the first step in the instructions was to plug the speaker into an outlet. I'm no electrician, but I believe that requirement exposed the "wireless" designation as a bald-faced lie. Step 2 was to establish the "wireless" connection between the soundbar and TV set. O…K… I guess that's what they were referring to on the package description. The soundbar and our TV were from the same manufacturer and the instructions indicated that any set produced by the company since 2012 had this feature built in to facilitate such a setup. I'd purchased our set in late 2013, right after we'd moved into our lake house, so I figured I was good to go. I figured wrong.

The TV did not have the "Sound Connect" feature as part of its array. Now I had to default to an alternate installation option, which specified the use of an "AUX Cable (not supplied)." Are you freaking KIDDING ME? After briefly flipping out, I noticed there was an optic cable included with the speaker which could be used as an alternate to the alternate. Huzzah.

Now all that was left to do was place the battery in the remote control (another remote control to add to my already impressive collection) and turn this sucker on. I pressed the power button and nothing happened. I continued to press the button, adding the "extend arm toward the device, using the elbow" motion as if I just needed to give the infrared impulse a little push to get it close enough to be recognized by the unit. Still no luck. I thought perhaps the battery was dead. Luckily I happened to have the same kind of pancake-shaped power source in my odds and ends box, so I swapped it out and tried again. Same outcome as Nixon's assessment of the results of the ten-year air campaign during the Vietnam War: "Zilch." I walked over and pressed the manual power switch I found on the front of the console; the display lit up and a few seconds later sound issued from the speaker. Utilizing my acute knowledge of home sound system manufacturing processes, I deduced the remote was defective. Crap.

Seeking a replacement, I called the manufacturer's toll-free customer service number and connected with a live representative after a shockingly minimal amount of menu navigation. The agent was very pleasant, empathizing with my issue and assuring me she could help resolve the matter quickly. She told me to remove the battery and then repeatedly press as many buttons on the remote as I could. I responded by assuring her I felt confident I could press all of the buttons — no technical novice was I. After doing so, she told me to reinsert the battery. Then she asked if I had a camera nearby — ??? Or did my smartphone have a camera built in — ??? Confused, I said my phone had a camera, whereupon she told me to point the remote at the phone while in camera mode and then press the power button. Ah, now I understood — this was a way for me to see if it was working without being blinded by whatever kind of pulse emanated from the device. I confirmed I saw flashing via the camera display, which pleased the rep. "Great!" she exclaimed. "Now we have confirmed that your remote is functioning properly. This means the receptor on your soundbar is defective. You can return it to our service center to have it repaired." I replied since I'd purchased the unit mere hours before, I would instead return it to the store for an exchange. Annoying, but quicker and easier than repackaging the unit, mailing it back to the company, and waiting weeks for its return.

Carol had been seated at the computer this whole time, close enough to hear the troubleshooting discussion. Once I'd hung up the phone and expressed my dismay at having purchased a bum speaker, she got up without a word and walked over to where I'd set it up in front of the TV. Giving it a quick once-over, she lifted the speaker and rotated it 90 degrees on its horizontal axis before setting it back down. "Try the remote again," she commanded. Shaking my head to imply, "Whatever…" I pressed the button, and the speaker immediately lit up. Speaking the words I was too dumbstruck to voice myself, Carol clarified I'd placed the speaker with its grill facing down rather than facing out from the TV (the manual controls were now displayed on the top, rather than the front, of the unit). Once the grill was in the correct alignment, the sensor was exposed, and everything worked as it should.

Except, of course, for my brain. That unit remains defective and, sadly, is long out of warranty.

Death Fakes a Holiday
(January 18, 2016)

Some years back, as we were watching TV one evening, my wife's ears suddenly pricked up and she leapt from the couch. "What's the matter?" I asked. "It's Josh," she replied. "He's crying." Apparently, he was howling at a frequency only a mother could hear.

Carol dashed upstairs, returning several minutes later with the nine-year-old Josh trailing behind, his face flushed, eyes wet, and using his pajama sleeve to wipe his tears and runny nose. Carol informed me Josh was upset about something and wanted to discuss it with both of us.

"What's the matter, buddy?" I asked, extending my arms and offering him a reassuring smile while trying to keep one eye on the courtroom histrionics unfolding during the second half of *Law & Order*. We discussed a concern common among children around his age — he had begun to wrestle with the concept of mortality.

Josh told us how he realized his grandparents were getting older and one day "soon" they would die, as would his parents and friends and pets. There was no reference to his own demise but I chose not to press him on that omission.

His mother and I took turns consoling him, trying to respond truthfully without introducing undue alarm. We trotted out all the usual homilies — death is a part of life, everybody/everything dies, it's not going to happen for a long time, yes we had named him as our sole beneficiary, etc. He eventually calmed down, seemingly placated by our reassurances, and soon went back to bed.

A few nights later, just as the late news came on, we heard footsteps and Josh came around the corner into the living room. Again he had been crying and was distraught. "What's wrong, honey?" his mother asked. He stopped sobbing long enough to exclaim, "It's death again!" We pulled him onto the couch between us and had a conversation very similar to the previous one. In between sniffles, he said his latest worry was around whether we were going to establish a living trust so he could avoid probate. I offered him a tissue, and while he blew his nose I said we'd certainly give it some thought.

The subject eventually faded from discussion, and the only other time after that I recall hearing Josh cry out in the middle of the night was about a year later. Carol and I dashed through the dark into his room to ask what was wrong. He was terrified because "There's a spider trying to kill me!" We said that was ridiculous and turned on the light so we could show him it was just his imagination. After flipping the switch, we saw a spider the size of a silver dollar descending from the ceiling light fixture along a thin line of silk, hovering inches from his face. It was a scene right out of a horror film, and all that was missing was a high-pitched shriek, which I obligingly provided. Carol, keeping her wits, ran to grab some toilet paper and quickly wrapped up the beast, relocating it to the commode and a swirling end of days. None of us, most importantly Josh, seemed upset in the least by how abruptly the spider had been forced to confront its mortality, and our son fell back asleep before inquiring as to the disposition of the arachnid's estate.

I thought of these vignettes after reading an article in our local newspaper about the sudden death of a man after shoveling snow. To clarify these events: both the man and I had recently shoveled snow; after that the man died, and after that I read about it. In the past when I'd heard about such tragedies, I didn't pay much attention since the decedent was usually someone well into middle age, older than me. But this time, I noticed the man was age 54; I had just turned 59. This gave me pause; I thought about my own mortality along with what I could do to make sure I didn't succumb to a similar fate from future attempts at this specific endeavor. I read an article about proper body mechanics when shoveling snow, reminders to pace oneself when doing so, and also considered whether it made sense to acquire a snow blower to lessen my exertion. I love to get a new toy as much as the next guy, but decent snow blowers are expensive — so I weighed my available options and return on investment while factoring in my blood pressure and cholesterol levels. After calculating the probabilities, I implemented the most effective course of action to all but guarantee I would never meet my demise as a result of shoveling snow.

I make Carol do it now.

Really in the Ears (with apologies to Steely Dan)
(January 31, 2017)

We were making idle chit-chat during dinner with friends, and I mentioned I'd be taking my car in for its 12,000-mile service. "But you just bought that car 7 months ago!" my wife Carol exclaimed. "How does it have 12,000 miles on it already?" "Well…," I replied cautiously, "that's because I've… driven it 12,000 miles since I purchased it." Carol looked at me intently and then said, *"Really?"*

A host of ripostes came to mind, most of which are not suited for a family audience, so I just chose to respond with, "Yes, really," and let the matter drop. But it was the latest example of Carol offering an incredulous response to something I've said that seems quite matter-of-fact to me. Here are some other examples:

- On a recent lazy Sunday afternoon, Carol mentioned she felt tired, and I encouraged her to take a nap. She agreed on the condition that I not let her sleep past 3 o'clock. At the appointed hour I went up to the bedroom and gently shook her shoulder while whispering in her ear: "Carol, it's time to get up… Honey, you said you didn't want to sleep any later than this." With her eyes still shut, she sleepily mumbled, "What time is it?" I said it was 3 o'clock. She opened her eyes, looked at me, and said, *"Really?"*
- I was watching the evening news while Carol finished making dinner. She called out to ask me what the next

day's weather was going to be. I said it was going to drop well below freezing. From the kitchen: *"Really?"*
- I reminded Carol that I'd be leaving early the next morning to go to the dentist for a cleaning. "Didn't you just go to the dentist?" I replied it had been six months since my last appointment, and now it was time for the next visit. *"Really?"*
- Carol was baking cookies and asked for my help in getting ingredients measured and ready to add. "OK, what's next?" she inquired. "Let's see…" I reviewed the recipe and said, "Next is a teaspoon of baking soda." "Baking soda? Why did you say 'baking soda'?" "Well… that's because the next ingredient listed here is 'baking soda'." *"Really?"*

And so on. Hardly a day goes by that at some point our conversation isn't peppered with a *"Really?"* Checking the time, mentioning we're out of peanut butter, reviewing the evening's TV listings ("Is there a new episode of *The Big Bang Theory* on tonight?" — "No, it's a rerun." — *"Really?"*). Now, from Carol's perspective this is just a conversational "tic," a form of benign acknowledgement; the equivalent of saying, "Oh!" or perhaps, "I didn't realize that." But to my ears (and psyche), I interpret this as her ongoing sense of disbelief in the veracity of whatever I am telling her at that moment. I think she thinks I don't know how to tell time, or how to read, or — in general — how to tell my ass from a hole in the ground.

My fear is that she will provide that same response when I need her to take immediate action related to an urgent request — such as:

- "Sweetheart, we need to leave right now or else we're going to miss the start of the movie." *"Really?"*
- "Honey, please don't flush the toilet while I'm taking a shower; the water gets scalding hot." *"Really?"*

- "CAROL! CALL 911 — I'VE SLICED MY ARM OFF WITH THE CHAIN SAW!" *"Really?"*

Now if I were to invite Carol to comment here, she'd likely say I'm exaggerating; stop it; I'm being ridiculous; of course she would attend to any medical emergency just as soon as she finished scrolling through the latest posts on her Facebook page.

I suppose I should be fair here. I imagine I have a behavioral tic, maybe even two, of my own that gets under Carol's skin. For example, I… uh, let's see — sometimes when I… hmm; nothing is coming to mind off the top of my head. As a matter of fact, as a result of this thought exercise I've come to the conclusion that I'm pretty damn terrific and Carol's lucky to have me as her husband, and I plan to tell her that. But I already know what her response will be:

"REALLY?"

My Bathroom Innovation Will Make You Flush with Excitement
(January 7, 2017)

"Honey," I say, taking my wife's hands in mine and looking into her eyes with all the affection I can muster, "I love you with all my heart. Keeping that in mind, I want to let you know the next time I go to use the bathroom and find a roll of toilet paper with only three sheets left on it — I'm leaving you."

She tells me she doesn't want to waste the remaining paper by throwing it out unused. I respond by asking what exactly can three sheets of toilet paper be used for? I suggest if thrift is her concern then perhaps she could use it to blow her nose, or remove some lipstick, or wipe the smudges off her phone screen and then install a fresh roll with a clear conscience. She says those all sound like silly suggestions to her. I offer another suggestion: if she doesn't come up with some solution — soon — then the next time this happens I will signal my displeasure by using those three sheets to start a small bonfire in the bathroom.

She says that's ridiculous. I counter that it's no more ridiculous than leaving a useless remnant of a toilet paper roll in place and expecting the next occupant to assume the responsibility for replacing it at a particularly inconvenient moment.

She says I'm not being fair; there are plenty of times when she finishes the roll and replaces it with a new one. I concede that *sometimes* she does that, but that leads to another concern: why do I find the empty cardboard center perched on the edge of the sink? "It's recyclable," she informs me. "Yes," I acknowledge. "I am well aware of that, and applaud you for your awareness of the environmental impact. But this is my question: how exactly do you expect that roll to be introduced into the Reuse-Reduce-Recycle triad without actually placing it in the recycling bin?"

She responds that she *intends* to place the empty roll in the recycling bin but occasionally just forgets. I remind her that the road to You Know Where (we used to say "Hell," but now we say "the Trump White House") is paved with good intentions. She looks at me with exasperation and asks why I am making such a big deal out of such a little thing. I say the future of our planet is not a "little thing." She tells me she's getting tired of dealing with my hyperbole. I tell her I'm getting tired of her unwillingness to consider how finding three useless sheets hanging limply, or a forlorn cardboard tube teetering on the edge of the sink, and then having to deal with those situations ON TOP OF everything else I am responsible for around the house drives me nuts.

Now the gloves come off. She asks me just WHAT exactly are all my "responsibilities" around the house? I start to tick off the list: empty the dishwasher, scoop out the cat litter, do all the laundry that's OK to go in the dryer, refill the bird feeders that she can't reach… I tell her I'm just providing the highlights here; there is more but at the moment I am too taken aback by her challenge to recite it all from memory. Then I offer this clincher: "There are LOTS of things I take care of that YOU WON'T HANDLE." A slight smirk slowly creases her face as she composes her response: "What exactly do you have to deal with that I can't take care of myself?" I look her straight in the eye and state, "I handle paying all the bills, and I file our taxes every year. I've never seen you even TRY to sign into our online banking or the tax program, much less take care of the monthly bills or our annual returns." She smacks herself in the forehead while rolling her eyes and says, "That's because you're the one who set up all the computer-based accounts WITHOUT TELLING ME WHAT ANY OF THE PASSWORDS ARE! I've asked you to write them down for me and you NEVER DO!" I inform her that writing down passwords is not a secure way to share them. I think I see a look of disbelief on her face just before she turns away from me. I realize that, correct as I may be, I have trod onto thin ice and attempt to gingerly work my way back to safer ground.

"Honey," I say, with all the affection I can muster, "I'm not trying to start an argument here."

"Oh, I think it's too late for that."

"Well… be that as it may. Let's see if we can come to an agreement — you accept your responsibility for replacing the toilet paper and getting the empty roll all the way into the recycling bin, and I'll promise to try and not shrink your yoga pants again. Doesn't that sound reasonable?"

She's been up in the bedroom with the door locked for several hours now, so she must be giving my proposal some serious thought. I've been using this time productively by unspooling all the rolls of toilet paper stored in the linen closet and writing "REMEMBER TO RECYCLE ME!" with a marker on the cardboard cores. I'm also reverse-numbering the corners of the sheets so it's clear when we get down to those last three useless squares. I just hope I can get all the paper wrapped back around the tubes before she comes downstairs. I can't wait to witness her response to my latest innovation in the name of household efficiency.

The Princess and the Pee Stain
(July 25, 2017)

Carol came downstairs this morning berating me, since she'd slipped on the path of rose petals I'd strewn along the steps to welcome her to the new day. You try to do something nice for someone… To her credit, she quickly got over her pique, stepping into my outstretched arms for a good morning hug. I then noticed she was wearing her pajamas inside-out. While I considered it unlikely that she'd had a romp with someone else while I was sleeping undisturbed (thanks to my earplugs) during the night, I did think it prudent to ask why her clothing was so arranged.

"It's because my skin is so sensitive — if I sleep with my pj's right-side out, the inside seams leave marks." I said that sounded ridiculous, so to prove her point Carol removed her pajama top to show me where she still had marks from not reversing her bedclothes before turning in several nights before. At least, I think that's what her intention was but I was focused on, shall we say, other desirable parts of her body that were now revealed.

Once I came out of my reverie, I saw reddened creases under her arms and along her sides. I offered a look of concern — briefly — and then, as is my wont, started in with the wisecracks:

- "If they made corduroy pajamas, you'd wake up looking like a Ruffles potato chip."
- "If I'd known you were that sensitive, I wouldn't have told you how stupid I thought *Under the Tuscan Sun* was."

131

- "The only other time something left that much of a painful impression on you was when you found out one of your yoga teachers was a Trump supporter."

I was coming up with some pretty funny zingers... well — *I* was laughing. Carol calmly went into the kitchen to get herself a cup of coffee while I continued riffing. When she returned, she took a sip from her cup and then said, "At least I don't have pee stains on the front of my pants when I come out from the bathroom."

A morning that only moments before had been warmed by mirth now turned icy cold. Carol's comment had wounded my soul, and I quickly ran through the Five Stages of Grief it had caused me:

- Denial — "I do <u>not</u> come out of the bathroom with pee stains on the front of my pants!"
- Anger — "I can't believe you would make fun of my incontinence issues."
- Bargaining — "If you'll lay off the insults, I'll go to another one of those idiotic 'mindfulness' seminars with you, OK?"
- Depression — "You have no idea how much I'm on edge every time I exit a public washroom."
- Acceptance — "I guess I could think about trying some 'adult' underwear..."

As I started to come out of my funk, I noticed Carol was snickering. "What's so amusing?" I asked. She finished sipping from her cup before responding, "Look who's sensitive <u>now</u>! I guess I'm not the only one with 'thin skin' around here."

After a few moments of contemplation, I forced a smile and said fair was fair — I'd landed the first blow, and she had only counter-punched in return. I apologized for my insensitive response to her dermatologic dismay, offering to make amends by going upstairs to strip the bed and remake it with fresh sheets while she relaxed over the rest of her coffee. She said that was very nice of me, taking a seat at the dining room table while I sprinted up to the bedroom to complete my penance.

It will be interesting tomorrow morning to see what her skin looks like after spending a night sleeping on luxurious, 400-thread-count Egyptian cotton sheets — under which, on her side of the mattress, I slid a piece of corrugated cardboard. Rest well, Your Highness!

Drain the Swamp
(October 21, 2017)

Carol woke me up at 4:00 this morning, saying it was time to get up and go out to get onion rings. I groggily rousted myself from the warm bed, pulled on my sweats, and stumbled down the stairs and outside to start the car. While I sat behind the wheel, waiting for Carol to come along, I opened the glove compartment to check on my emergency stash of ketchup packets. It would be a shame to head out for onion rings at that hour and not have the proper condiments at hand.

I saw Carol exit the house in the glare of the headlights. With a puzzled look on her face, she walked over and pulled open the driver's side door. "What the hell are you doing?" I explained I was preparing to drive us to whatever diner was open at this ungodly hour to obtain some onion rings. She laughed and shook her head — "No… I said it was time to get up to go out and see the Orionid meteor shower." That made even less sense to me than going on a pre-dawn diner run.

As I continued to clear the fog from my head, I recalled that we'd agreed to set an alarm and get up while it was still dark to see if we could spy any of the remnants from Halley's Comet that were streaking through the atmosphere, with the peak viewing period being in the wee hours over the weekend. I turned off the engine, pulling ketchup packets out of my pockets to return to their secure location in the glove box. Stumbling out of the car, I followed Carol into the yard to a spot for the viewing.

We settled back into our recliners, turning our gaze toward the heavens. Experts say it takes twenty minutes for your eyes to adjust to the dark, which is coincidentally the same amount of time I can sit outside in the cold before needing to pee. Now I faced a dilemma: would I go inside to use the bathroom, meaning I'd have to flick on a blinding light to make sure I hit the bowl and therefore need to reacclimate my vision — or would I take care of business outdoors so my pupils, now as large as the hamburger I apparently was not going to be ordering with that side of onion rings, could remain adjusted to the dark? I opted to stay outside and so took some cautious steps toward the edge of the yard in order to find a place to relieve myself.

"I think I just heard the splash of the Canada geese landing on the lake!" Carol called out. But she was mistaken — what she'd heard was the splash of a vertiginous American male tripping over a tree root and tumbling ass over teakettle into the marshy field bordering our property line. I emerged from the swamp looking like… something emerging from a swamp. Damp, muddy, vegetation dripping from my shoulders; all I lacked were gills and scales. I shook off some of the wetness and removed as much of the detritus from my clothing as I could before returning to my seat next to Carol. "What's that smell?" she asked, unable to see my aqueous appearance in the darkness. I replied it was the smell of despair mixed with exhaustion and a soupçon of dead fish. "Whatever," she responded after a brief hesitation and then asked, "Have you seen any meteors yet? Have you? Where are you? Are you on your way back to bed?"

No — I was on my way to Denny's for those onion rings and a milkshake. And a whole lot of napkins.

Dogged by a Pet Name
(January 4, 2018)

My wife Carol has a pet name for me — but it's not what you are thinking. I'll show respect for the family audience and won't spell it out here, but it's seven letters, starting with "a" and ending with "e."

Oh, wow — you came up with it right away. I guess it *is* what you were thinking. My bad.

Anyway… now that you know the name, I trust you'll believe me when I say she uses it affectionately. Most of the time. She'll use it in a playfully teasing way when we banter over some minor transgression. Here are some sample exchanges:

CAROL: "I'll be ready to leave as soon as I put on my makeup."
ME: "So — you'll be another forty-five minutes, then?"
CAROL: "Lay off, [pet name]."

CAROL: "How many times do I have to tell you — my yoga pants do not go in the dryer!"
ME: "I guess you should have told me at least one more time."
CAROL: "Really, [pet name]?"

CAROL: "Could you take this package to the post office for me?"
ME: "Sure. What should I do with it once I get there?"
CAROL: "You are an unbelievable [pet name]."

It may seem a little harsh out of context, but if you could hear her tone and see her expression… Well, I guess "harsh" is probably a correct assessment.

As you may have surmised from the dialogue above, she tends to ~~bellow~~ coo my pet name in response to something I've done that, perhaps, was not quite up to her standards. The laundry, for instance — or I've paid the bills online, but I've transposed the numbers and now our checking account is overdrawn by $10,000

— or I've made her half a peanut butter and jelly sandwich to take to work for lunch but instead of cutting one slice of bread in two, I've made it open-faced and forgot to wrap it up and she's found the condiments smeared all over the inside of her tote bag. But don't you think if you do something nice for someone, they should be appreciative of the effort — even if it's not your best effort?

I know she really doesn't mean anything by it, but I have to admit it does get under my skin on occasion. When I'm feeling that way, I take a deep breath, remind myself of the old adage regarding sticks and stones, and then "accidentally" toss her chiffon blouse in with my sweaty t-shirts.

Sometimes, I can be a real [petname].

Teller I Love Her
(March 10, 2019)

Last week I sat down to pay our monthly bills via the online banking portal, as I've been doing for well over a decade. I really can't recall the last time I wrote a check to settle a financial transaction. (I understand Donald Trump suffers from a similar malady.)

Cable, cellphone, credit cards, car payment (and that's just the "C"s) – pretty much everything other than the grocery bill (which, come to think of it, we use a dedicated credit card for and pay off that balance online) – I check all the monthly statements on the web, log into our bank's site, copy and paste the amounts due, and schedule when the funds should be released. It's a simple, efficient process, and I don't have to pay for postage or keep a fat accordion file of canceled checks to thumb through in the event of a dispute. Easy-peasy.

At least... until the other day. I logged into the bank account to confirm all payments had been made according to schedule and saw that $170.84 had been paid to one of the credit cards. The problem: it was for a credit card we hadn't used in well over a year; there were no recent charges or outstanding balance. I was befuddled and couldn't make sense of what had gone awry, so I clicked the chat icon on the bank's webpage and waited for "Cassie" to enter the conversation in approximately 3 minutes.

I should mention here that I rarely speak to any service representatives over the phone anymore. If there's an email or chat option to contact a business – I'll eagerly make use of it rather than feel forced to engage in conversation with a total stranger. Besides having the advantage of providing a written trail of the interaction in the event of a misunderstanding or dispute, permitting myself the luxury of typing out my answers allows me to "speak" in complete, coherent sentences, saying precisely what I mean and without the other party being subjected to how tongue-tied and red in the face I get every time I open my mouth in real life.

Once Cassie popped into the chat window with her pre-programmed greeting, I quickly qwerty'd my inquiry regarding the obviously fraudulent payment. She asked if I'd mind holding while she researched, and after the briefest of pauses came back to inform me that I'd entered the payment request on the 4th of the month and it was processed on the 7th. "Yes," I typed in response, "I understand the dates involved but would not have sent a payment to that particular credit card company since there was no balance due." I hit "enter" and waited for Cassie to respond with further insight.

After a minute, I saw a prompt appear: *"Cassie is typing…"* "A-ha," I thought to myself, "she's found the error and is about to tell me she's returning the funds to my account. Mystery solved!" In fact, I can refer to the log of the chat session to let you know her exact words – which were, "John, are you still there?" We then got involved in an extended back-and-forth where I kept aggressively insisting I'd authorized no such payment, and Cassie kept politely insinuating I didn't know my ass from a hole in the ground (I'm paraphrasing here rather than quoting from the transcript).

I was getting increasingly frustrated and told Cassie I was going to double-check my own display of the payment history. I went back to that tab in the browser, preparing to arm myself with the final piece of incontrovertible evidence to put Cassie in her place and prevail over the banking-industrial complex. As I reviewed the bill pay page, I found the problem: I had sent money intended to pay one bill (the cable company, starting with "S") to the next payee listed in alphabetical order on the page (the credit card company, starting with "T"). I had, if this phrase is still part of the vernacular, "fat-fingered" the entry and was entirely to blame for the kerfuffle.

I sheepishly returned to the chat session (dammit... I managed to get red-faced even while avoiding personal contact) and informed Cassie of my discovery. I apologized and then asked if she could assist in recovering the misapplied funds and have them returned to my account. Unfortunately, she typed, she was unable to do that since the payment had already been processed. I would need to contact the company myself to make that request, and I'd have to wait another 2-3 business days before the payment would show up in their records.

Arrgh... I was already imagining how convoluted that process was going to be, anticipating a laborious series of interactions requiring several levels of approval and weeks of processing time. Meanwhile, I still had to pay the cable bill from our remaining funds while the same amount of money would languish indefinitely in the cold, interest-free hands of the credit card company. I exited my chat with Cassie (who, I'm certain, leaned over to the virtual teller in the next cubicle to share: *"You wouldn't BELIEVE the recalcitrant cretin I just dealt with!"*) and made a reminder on my phone calendar to make contact after the waiting period.

That evening, I told my wife Carol what had transpired, leaving no detail out of the story and reading occasionally from the chat session transcript to provide notes of dramatic vérité to the retelling. She, to her credit, remained generally attentive as my recounting passed the 30-minute mark. In my version of events, I lamented over the inevitable difficulty of dealing with a corporate behemoth and getting the funds returned in anything remotely resembling a reasonable time frame. I'll take care of it, but woe is me and all that mishegas.

When I finally wrapped up my narrative, providing an opportunity for Carol to offer soothing words of empathy and compassion, she responded with: "Can't you just use that credit card to pay the cable bill this month? Then you'll have paid the bill and used the credit balance on the card without creating any further hassle for yourself."

An awkward moment of silent contemplation – as the crimson rose from my neck to the top of my head – and then I provided the only appropriate response under the circumstances: "Fine, then – YOU can take care of paying the bills from now on!"

No, not really – I thanked Carol for identifying a simple, expedient solution to the matter at hand, admitting how chagrinned I was that I hadn't thought of it first. I then logged back into the bank's website, opened a new chat session, solicited Cassie's return, relinquished my seat at the computer to Carol, and let the two of them commiserate over what a moron I am. There's no doubt in my mind Carol requested a copy of *that* transcript.

Brow Beaten
(February 24, 2022)

After a recent cut-and-color, my wife mentioned she would be heading back to the salon within a few days to have her "eyebrows done." Since her regular styling costs a C-note, I figured just the brows could be groomed for maybe ten bucks. Imagine my shock when she said the procedure would set us back a cool five-hundred smackers.

"Good God!" I exclaimed. "Is that PER EYEBROW?" She replied that was the cost to have both of them shaped and tattooed. "You're getting a TATTOO? On your FACE?" I envisioned some sort of tribal design, à la Mike Tyson, wondering if there was a filter on my phone's camera that could magically erase it when we posed for a selfie.

She brought up a video of the process, known as "microblading," which looked to me like she'd willingly be paying to experience death by a thousand cosmetic cuts. The benefit, she explained, was she would no longer need to spend precious seconds each day filling in her eyebrows with a pencil since the results were permanent. Or, as she clarified, "semi-permanent."

"What do you mean by 'semi-permanent'? There is either 'permanent' or 'temporary' – there is no in-between." Such a statement delivered by Yoda might sound profound, but from my lips – not so much. I saw her trying to stifle a yawn.

I then decided to point out the potential risks of this endeavor: "What if the person doing the tattooing gets the hiccups? Or they're inspired by Frida Kahlo's appearance and you end up with a unibrow? And could you have that done for half price?"

In response, she offered a look suggesting, "I've had enough of your gibberish." Realizing I could not talk her out of the decision, I offered a mumbled, "Whatever makes you happy." An ardent feminist would have stood squarely behind, "Her eyebrows – her choice." I, however, felt the need to re-establish equilibrium in our relationship and decided if she could spend $500 on body art – then so could I.

The day she returned to the salon, I hightailed it over to an area tattoo parlor, handing over a rough sketch of what I'd envisioned. I spent the next two hours nearly biting through my lower lip.

Once we were both back home, she asked what I thought of her enhanced eyebrows. "Nice enough," I replied, "… but what do you think about THIS?" I dropped my drawers to reveal my ink work. Since I couldn't see her reaction, I explained, "It's a heart – to show my love for you."

She responded, "I can see it's a heart – but why does it look broken?"

"Oh, that," I sighed. "Unfortunately, the guy got the hiccups."

New Skin off my Nose
(March 23, 2022)

For the second year in a row, my dermatologist identified two small skin cancers – one on my left nostril (mirroring a basal cell lesion found the year before on the right side of my nose) and the other on my left thigh (a small squamous cell nodule). Both were caught relatively early and neither was particularly deep, so their removal the other day was quick and only minimally disfiguring.

The worst part of the procedure was the administration of the anesthetic – if you've never had a needle jabbed repeatedly into the fleshy part of your schnozz, I don't suggest you volunteer for the experience. But once my nose, and later my thigh, were properly numbed, the actual surgery took mere minutes and generated discomfort only when the wounds were cauterized to prevent bleeding and I could smell my own burning flesh.

My wife Carol accompanied me for moral support. Afterward, she drove us home from the operation – not that I was discombobulated in any way, but mostly because I had a pressure bandage bulging out from one side of my face and couldn't have seen any traffic approaching from the left. Since the appointment had been first thing in the morning, we'd skipped making coffee at home and planned to stop on our way back at an outlet of a local convenience store chain that offers fresh, hot coffee for the ridiculous price of 99 cents, regardless of cup size.

Once we'd pulled into the lot, I offered to hop out and get our drinks. I put on my KN95 mask – partly because we're still being cautious amidst the pandemic, but mostly because it hid my bandaging from public view – and dashed inside to obtain our extra-large caffeine fixes. I take my coffee black (as God intended), and added a splash of cream to Carol's because she, apparently, is an atheist. I picked up the two containers, but before I could move them to the counter in order to secure the lids, my glasses began to slide off my face due to the mask's slippery earloops. I threw my head back to try and keep my glasses from falling to the floor; my extended arms followed suit and I spilled several ounces of Carol's still-blistering hot coffee all over my right hand.

While contemplating whether I'd need to return to the dermatologist's office for an emergency skin graft, I added some additional brew to Carol's cup and then, regrettably a tad too late, affixed the lids and paid at the checkout. I brought them out to the car; Carol cracked a window so I could hand hers over. I slipped into the passenger seat clutching my beverage and saw Carol examining her cup, which still had some traces of coffee dripping down its sides. I explained what had happened: how I had very nearly lost a substantial portion of the flesh covering my dominant hand and, in my agony, had only been able to pay minimal attention to the extent of any mop-up effort. Carol removed the lid from her drink to inspect it and then informed me that, "for future reference," she preferred it with more cream.

Fighting to hold back tears as my skin began to blister, I thanked her for clarifying how she takes her coffee and promised that, if I ever were to regain full use of my right hand, I would add enough cream to subsequent pours to meet her exacting standards.

Settling into my seat, I folded back the little tab atop the lid and brought the fragrant brew to my lips just as Carol left the parking lot to accelerate into traffic. Now my throbbing hand was paired with blistered lips and chin as the scalding beverage splashed onto my face. The boiling liquid also soaked my shirt sufficiently to generate a second-degree burn on my chest.

The lesson I learned from all this: the potential for future, painful consequences means you should never skip the application of sunscreen. Also – there's nothing wrong with iced coffee in the morning.

Stairing Contest
(May 18, 2022)

Well, despite the proverbial "abundance of caution" (over two years' worth!) – and even after the second round of booster shots – Carol and I recently managed to test positive for Covid. Bummer.

While Carol's bout was not severe enough to require hospitalization, she experienced nearly the full array of symptoms: fever, congestion, unrelenting cough, head and body aches, profound *ennui*. As for myself – I lost four pounds.

Oh, not because I was suffering from those same symptoms; I lost the weight from running up and down the stairs to our bedroom where Carol was isolated for a whole week, bringing her cough drops, tissues, decongestant, more tissues, meals, hot tea, still more tissues… I tested positive two days after Carol did, but by then the die had been cast (not that anybody died), and I was in the role of "providing for" rather than "suffering from."

I was fortunate to experience only a mild manifestation of short duration; just one day where I felt like absolute crap, but afterward I bounced back to my usual curmudgeonly self. Our son did his best to keep himself tucked away throughout the ordeal and managed to remain unafflicted. He took care of his own needs while maintaining as much distance from his ailing mother and virus-shedding father as he could in our modest, two-bedroom home.

However, his approach meant the caregiver responsibilities were mine and mine alone. I handled cooking (all), cleaning (minimal), and laundry (even less than). I slept downstairs in the living room on the inflatable mattress, which required re-inflating several times per night to prevent severe sagging. I put a mask on and off more times than Zorro during hay fever season.

Here I must confess that despite my banishment from our bedroom – I did not sleep alone. I was joined by our two cats, Nate and Miles, who spent most evenings curled up on the blanket next to me, rousing only long enough to deposit hairballs near my face or use the mattress as a scratching pad (perhaps that's why it required so much re-inflation). Cats are just awesome and we have two currently up for adoption.

Carol obtained a prescription for antiviral medication, which we presume lessened the severity and duration of her symptoms but didn't cut down much on the extent of her kvetching. Day 10 of the Covid challenge brought the first negative test result – Carol's. However, she's still recovering slowly from the exhaustion, and so I continue with most of the household duties while she rests to regain her strength while watching hours of Netflix programming wherein medievals who all speak with English accents, regardless of their nationality, have prodigious amounts of sex in-between slaying one another.

I've continued to test positive but am bothered only by the resentment I feel at not being the coddled one. Carol has thanked me multiple times for my good husbandry, promising she'll make it all up to me once she feels back to normal.

While that's kind of her, I'm not certain if she means the "old" or the "new" normal. Either way – I suspect I can hasten her return to productivity by conveniently "forgetting" what I've changed the Netflix password to.

Rhymes A-Wastin' (Part II)

Once Trump departed for Mar-A-Lardo, I largely took a respite from the political realm but still felt a need to scratch the rhyme itch. My focus for most of the next year was on devising short, light verses about various oddities in the news (other than Trump) – stories that made the various wire services about animals, medicine, food, unusual behaviors (other than Trump's) – along with the occasional humor essay, some of which may have found their way into other sections of this book. I had set up <u>Rhyme for the News</u> a few years before but was now making more regular contributions to that site. Here's a smattering from the hundred or so I've posted so far.

Cereal Killer
(October 25, 2018)

A weed (and appetite?) killer was found in some of your favorite breakfast foods.

They say to cut back sugar in your morning breakfast bowl,
and substitute some whole grains for that frosted cinnamon roll.
But now there's an ingredient whose presence has me wound up –
instead of added vitamins, my cereal's got Roundup®.

I sure was not expecting to find glyphosate in cereal;
it's like sitting on a toilet, then contracting ills venereal.
Nobody wants to sit down to a helping of carcinogen –
I'll have to change the menu so my diet can begin again.

Of course the manufacturers provide a ready answer:
there's no need to be worried, and don't even speak of cancer.
I'm trying to stay calm and not respond with a hair trigger, yet
from now on I'll spend mornings with just coffee and a cigarette.

Tüber
(December 5, 2018)

A Harvard professor recommends no more than six French fries per serving.

According to an expert, our choice to fry a spud
in tasty, slender, salted strips is something of a dud.
A serving size of six is all this fellow is proposing,
which hardly seems enough to satisfy my French fry jonesing.

Honestly, this shouldn't come as much of a surprise,
considering what else we tend to eat with our French fries:
a juicy, fat-filled burger, and a rich and creamy shake,
and afterwards, we run the risk the bathroom scale may break.

The willpower necessary to adhere to this amount
means while we're pigging out, we also have to keep a count.
This Harvard prof may think we are impressed with his diploma
–
but no way I'll do math while slipping into a food coma.

Repast Due
(November 21, 2019)

It gets harder to set a holiday table with each passing year…

Thanksgiving's just around the corner;
called my mom, so I could warn her
I no longer find prestige in
eating turkey – now I'm vegan.

Mushrooms can't have sausage stuffing.
Yams: without marshmallow fluff. String
beans are fine without the butter
(nothing that comes from an udder).

Gingered carrots can't have honey.
Bacon-wrapped dates? Won't eat one. We
need to focus more on plant-based;
screw those deviled eggs from Aunt Grace.

Everyone will hate me when you
tell them how I trashed your menu.
Tension's surely gonna thicken
once they learn I'm also Wiccan.

Birder Most Fowl
(January 26, 2021)

A famous Florida city considers fines to curb the feeding of wild chickens.

Some chickens – they're feral – roam free in Key West.
A risk they'll imperil now must be addressed.
They're fed by the tourists since they are free-roaming,
an action the town says it can't be condoning.

The problem the city now faces is whether
to fine those who feed these birds festooned with feathers.
They're sometimes fed popcorn, and other times French fries,
which spawns a big mess, and a huge fowl-percent rise.

The place Ernest Hemingway once knew as home
is now where these chickens (and six-toed cats) roam.
The challenge presented to vexed civic boosters
is how to defend against ambush by roosters.

To others, it may appear somewhat absurd
legislation's required, just for feeding a bird.
If this effort so poultry will not run amok
is enforced – it's the chickens who won't give a cluck.

Spritz Impossible
(February 9, 2021)

A woman mistakenly cements her hair by using a permanent adhesive.

I'm no expert on most things tonsorial, but may I dare say:
you should never, ever use Gorilla Glue in place of hairspray.
When your hair needs holding power, Aqua Net is recommended.
Glue comes with a warning label: "For Use Only As Intended."

Running out of product that a woman used to tend her coif,
she substituted glue – and now she cannot get the damn stuff off.
It doesn't matter if she used a lot, or squirted just a smidge:
when running low on aerosol, don't substitute with mucilage.

It's been a month so far and still the woman can't remove the glue.
Perhaps it comes as no surprise the next step is: she says she'll sue.
Among the styling tips acknowledged as hair-dressing orthodoxy,
no beautician's known to say, "When out of hair spray, use epoxy."

Hexed Libris
(February 25, 2021)

Discovery of a pernicious pest forced the closure of a university library.

Most people aren't worried, when taking out books,
that arachnids are hiding in crannies and nooks.
The place you'll find students on term papers working
is where you might least expect spiders are lurking.

A Michigan library, to their chagrin,
found that they'd been invaded by bugs; ones that spin

sticky webs, which don't normally scare girls and boys when
encountered – unless they are loaded with poison.

An insect has six legs, a spider has eight –
but who's counting when venom is sealing your fate?
A leisurely stroll through the library stacks
should be largely precluded from spider attacks.

An effort was made that should at best console
those who find reassurance in strict pest control.
The risk of a bite should be infinitesimal
when browsing the system known as Dewey Decimal.

Schmooze Operator
(March 3, 2021)

A medical professional seemed to lose focus during a procedure.

The jurist of a traffic court was really not enthused
by the actions that an M.D. took; the platform that he used –
since a medico's attention (all of it, one might assume)
should be on the patient underneath the knife, and not on Zoom.

A plastic surgeon (certainly for trouble he was asking)
picked the wrong time to show off his aptitude for multi-tasking.
Irregardless of however he's maneuvered in the past, he
shouldn't make a court appearance on a screen mid-rhinoplasty.

You don't expect to see while you lay prostrate on a gurney
your physician, at the same time, function as his own attorney.
The expectation is your doctor probes your organs tenderly
and doesn't choose to step away to plead nolo contendere.

As hair plugs are implanted so your bald spot is concealed,
there should be no litigation that concerns failure to yield.

Docs should give Botox injections in a method quite particular
without being distracted by infractions; type: vehicular.

A surgeon should move quickly when he sees that you are bleeding
but not stop your operation to explain why he was speeding.
So the judge shut down the doctor's trial, and sternly chose to warn him –
and thank goodness that this patient's loved ones didn't have to mourn him.

Grand Canal Seizure
(March 28, 2021)

A plan to slip through a narrow channel has gone sideways.

A big cargo ship's gotten stuck in the Suez
(perhaps you've seen pictures of this on the new-ez).
The ship's quite large; shows up on satellite view-ez.
The wake it creates would tip over canoe-ez.

As all other vessels are blocked, in long queu-ez,
this gives shipping companies angst and the blu-ez.
The wind was first blamed – but there's some who accu-ez
the captain, with thoughts he was taking a snoo-ez.

The leader of Egypt has got a short fu-ez
and will not accept any further miscu-ez.
What once seemed comedic now does not amu-ez.
With worldwide supply chains this mishap sure screw-ez.

Crash Decision
(April 3, 2021)

A sophisticated analysis forestalls the risk posed by a heavenly body.

Most of us living all have pasts devoid
of being concerned about asteroids.
A new NASA forecast has now blunted fears:
no chance we'll be struck for the next hundred years.

The thought of collision gives one pause; it shocks
to think there's any chance that a huge cosmic rock
might slam into Earth while we still live upon it.
Fat chance we'd survive a celestial bomb hit.

This asteroid, given the Greek name Apophis,
could possibly strike where the Arc de Triomphe is.
Wherever it lands would be marked with a placard.
(The worst place, of course, would be right in your backyard.)
Some people are anxious, perhaps could lose sleep:
our planet might one day be a refuse heap.
But now that we know it's unlikely to happen
while we're still alive – let's all get back to nappin'.

House of Buggin'
(May 7, 2021)

Parts of the country are preparing for a periodic invasion.

Cicadas are soon to emerge, by the trillions.
Upwards from down below earth they will spill, then
start shedding their skins, and their wings will unfurl.
The purpose: for boys to knock boots with the girls.

After seventeen years, they have grown into nymphs.
It takes all this time before we get a glimpse

of what they have evolved into, prior to molting:
Non-entomologists find it revolting.

What purpose is served by the homely cicada?
They prune mature trees, and they also aerate the
soil from which they came for their cyclic arrival.
But why are there trillions? Best odds for survival.

People seem scared, but they shouldn't be frightened;
so what if these horny bugs have sex all night, and
the noise they make equals a rock band (electrified)?
Please, just let them be: there's no need for insecticide.

Special Saucer
(May 22, 2021)

The truth may be out there – depending upon what a pending government analysis has to say.

All of a sudden, reports have intensified
as concern objects that fly, unidentified.
There's a new label that's now much more common: a
move to drop "Object" – instead, use "Phenomena."

Crack Navy pilots have spent much time tailing them;
still there's debate whether earth-bound or alien.
Now we await a report – any day –
to confirm if they're actual, or *trompe l'oeil*.

It's a surprise that the Pentagon's cast aside
prior restrictions and now has declassified
videos showing flight patterns mysterious.
What was once laughed at is now taken serious.

Call them a UFO or UAP –
are they outer space saucers, or hyperbole?
Some believe they exist; some say, "Give it a rest." We will
see if there's proof that they're extraterrestrial.

Marching Madness
(June 4, 2021)

Some of the largest land mammals on Earth are lumbering unsupervised.

Have you ever seen an elephant (or, let me use a fancy term –
among the *cognoscenti*, it's referred to as a pachyderm)?
Perhaps you've met one at a zoo, and even touched its skin, so
there's a chance you might not freak out if you saw one out your
window.

But a herd in southwest China, who broke free from a reserve,
have shown up in people's farmlands – leaving residents
unnerved.
They are known for giant flat feet, and their girth is rather ample,
so it comes as no surprise as they pass through that crops are
trampled.

They have traveled several hundred miles, through territory rural.
Why they broke out is unclear; perhaps to give free-range a whirl.
One of them ate some fermented fruit and possibly got drunk –
so
please be careful, keep your distance: you had best avoid this
trunk show.

Getting Over the Humpback
(June 16, 2021)

A commercial fisherman survived an Old Testament experience.

Jonah: swallowed by a whale –
so goes that ancient Bible tale.
Three days spent in the beast's intestine
(must've caused great indigestion).

Now we hear a lobster diver
is the latest whale survivor.
Swallowed whole – but soon expelled.
(Inside of there, I bet it smelled.)

Those people who in theory were
within a whale's interior
have quite a yarn to spin once spewed
and found not suitable as food.

A whale's a mammal, as you know –
warm-blooded; they breathe air – and so
despite what certain skeptics wish, we
can't say this account sounds fishy.

Let's Be Frankfurter
(July 9, 2021)

Speaking of conspicuous consumption...

A woman ate hot dogs, all slathered in chili;
in 22 minutes – this sounds rather silly –
she'd managed to chow down (uncertain for whose sake)
a total of 50 of these spruced-up tube steaks.

This person's an eater, the kind called "competitive" –
who somehow wins prizes for feasting repetitive.
While most of us, modestly, might ask for seconds,
these champion eaters say piles of food beckons.

Cholesterol levels: a hundred-percent rise;
perhaps even more if each frank came with French fries.
(If I eat <u>three</u> hot dogs I have to unbutton
my trousers – yet all *I'll* be called is a glutton.)

The call to consume for these eaters is clarion.
They mostly eat meat (just a few vegetarian).
It matters not whether you fry, bake, or boil it:
[insert your own joke here involving a toilet.]

Here's the Scoop
(July 24, 2021)

A new concoction delivers a double-whammy to the lactose-intolerant.

Ice cream's a treat almost everyone savors,
a frozen concoction that's likely to please.
And now you can add to the list of its flavors
a dish made from Kraft Macaroni & Cheese.

We've heard parents say, "No dessert without eating
what's served on your dinner plate – <u>all</u> of the food groups!"
So this is a way kids comply without cheating:
main course and dessert served together, in two scoops.

For those who prefer that their ice cream's traditional,
this mac and cheese flavor may not seem a fun one.
Perhaps we will soon see, with claims it's nutritional,
a pint of mint chip – mixed with liver and onion.

Running Short
(October 2, 2021)

Just because you cross the finish line first doesn't always mean you've won the race.

I've never run a marathon, but if I choose to do so,
I won't set any records, since my plodding would be too slow.
A race that long, with twists and turns, I'd surely find confusing;
no chance that I'd win, place or show – just merely end up losing.

Two runners in a recent race, who both had much experience,
diverted off the proper course. Perhaps they'd gotten weary, since
a marathon goes on for many miles, with pace unflagging.
It seems these fellows zigged when they should really have been zagging.

They both were well ahead; had run a little more than halfway –
but then a biking volunteer steered them down the wrong pathway.
The runner in the third-place slot stayed on the straight and narrow,
which meant he was awarded the blue ribbon, plus *dinero*.

The runners who veered off the course were very clearly shaken;
regrettable the road they took they both should not have taken.
If there's a lesson to be learned, it's just as Robert Frost said:
whichever road you choose, the choice will leave you quite exhausted.

Presents Aren't Accounted For
(November 9, 2021)

Global events can't cancel – but may alter – how some choose to celebrate the holidays.

It's another Covid Christmas – Santa can't come down the chimney
unless he's been vaccinated and he has a mask on him. He's
being hounded by the elves, who won't agree to vaccination.
(There's no mandate at the North Pole, much to St. Nick's
consternation.)

Mrs. Claus, a vaccine-backer, has cajoled the anti-vaxxers,
but the elves are not persuaded by this cavalcade of facts. Her
valiant efforts all for naught, and Santa Claus is disappointed
when the sprites stick fingers in their ears (which, you'll recall, are
pointed).

Toy production has been slowed, due to concerns with the
supply chain.
Tracking shifting shipping timelines now gives Santa Claus a
migraine.
Fill-in labor means the quality of goods is less meticulous.
It's not looking good this season for the bounty from Saint
Nicholas.

And it isn't only Christmas; this kerfuffle also spawns a
big concern regarding celebrating Hanukkah and Kwanzaa.
Acquisition versus Thankfulness: an old, eternal schism.
So – perhaps we should dial back the focus on commercialism.

River-Horsing Around
(November 13, 2021)

Steps are being taken to limit any further population growth of a mammoth mammal.

Here's a dicey topic one ignores and not discusses:
birth control administered to hippotamuses.
There are several methods (none relying on a condom;
that's a risky effort if you've tried to slip one on some).

Hippos in Colombia – brought in by Pablo Escobar;
derelict herd management's allowed them to progress so far.
Starting from just four, left to their own they chose to multiply.
(If you stick with Latin, then the plural's "hippopotami.")

Every single hippo turned a deaf ear to entreaties:
"Abstinence is best!" Now, they're a large, invasive species.
Forced sterilization curbs the numbers, ipso facto.
Careful family planning is a skill most hippos lack, though.

Hook, Line and Blinker
(January 12, 2022)

A common household pet can acquire an astounding skill.

Though chimps fulfilled a bold wish
and flew rockets toward the stars,
it's still shocking to learn goldfish
have been trained to drive a car.

Horses do addition,
and some dogs have learned to speak.
But you don't expect when fishin'
to see trout park near the creek.

Elephants do paintings,
and a crow can hold a grudge –
whereas people do mundane things.
Should fish drive? I won't begrudge.

No need to be wary
and, in fact, we should give thanks:
fish could join the military –
since they learn by driving tanks.

Casting a Spell
(January 22, 2022)

It's the latest craze that's gone viral.

It seems everybody is now playing Wordle,
a spelling game online, with one simple hurdle:
take turns trying to suss out a five-letter word
(a few of which you may not ever have heard).

You must guess successfully by your sixth try.
First, focus on vowels: a-e-i-o-u; why?
What helps: "sound it out" with each subsequent turn.
(The word that I most like to start with is "urine.")

The rules are quite simple, not many components;
there aren't any clocks or obnoxious opponents.
The answers all live in the encyclopedia.
(Some post their results on preferred social media.)

A colored square fills in behind each typed letter.
Gray's bad, yellow's good, but a green one is better.
Each letter may be utilized more than once.
(If you need all six tries, you're kind of a dunce.)

A pleasant time-waster, a morsel of brain food,
a wee bit of strategy useful to play shrewd.
It's pretty straightforward, and so won't exhaust nerds
not up to the challenge of New York Times crosswords.

Creepy Sleepytime
(January 30, 2022)

A dip in the jet stream may cause an astonishing phenomenon in Florida.

Cold temps can be taxing to flora and fauna –
particularly, if you are an iguana.
Although they're cold-blooded, it's known that a freeze
can cause tropical lizards to fall out of trees.

It isn't a spectacle you'd expect daily
while walking in Florida, as something scaly
cascades from a branch; an unusual burden for
what is an otherwise settled-in herbivore.

Florida's known for the warmth of its sunshine,
and yet this has happened before, more than one time.
A strange quirk of nature for someone to witness –
if I saw this happening, I'd be scared shitless.

Spread Alert
(February 26, 2022)

A coveted comestible is conspicuously absent from the dairy case.

There's a short supply of cream cheese;
you can search both far and near.
Bagel lovers now all scream, "These
deli favorites need a schmear!"

Whether spreadable or brick-style,
its devoted clientele
have exhausted every trick, while
settling for Neufchâtel.

Needed for a cream cheese frosting
or a cheesecake that's divine.
Yet no matter what it's costing –
devotees will stand in line.

Used in jalapeño poppers
or a filling for a blintz,
it's been filched by savvy shoppers –
others haven't seen it since.

Though this issue may seem frivolous
it's a fact that cream cheese rocks!
Gustatory pleasure given us;
best of all – when paired with lox.

Come and Flamingo
(April 2, 2022)

Something escaped confinement — yet isn't considered a fugitive.

Some years back, a pink flamingo
dwelled within a Kansas zoo.
Seems they never clipped its wings, so
out amidst a storm it flew.
Once escaping from confinement
(joined by yet another bird),
it soared far, across state lines – went
all directions, so we've heard.

This bird spent time in Wisconsin;
a Louisiana perch;
it's quite clear this fowl began a
quest for peace – a tiresome search.
Currently, it's found in Texas
where it likes to socialize.
As to what this bird expects: it's
fellowship – that's no surprise.
Living life free and unfettered,
as compared to vassalage,
is the best idea yet heard:
home is where your castle is.

A-Peel-ing Behavior
(April 10, 2022)

Scientists anticipate the onset of the singularity will encompass a well-balanced diet.

Of all of the tasks that we often find tedious,
the worst are those tied into mealtime and feeding – thus
let's automate kitchen labors. Or so thought
some techie-types: "Peeling bananas by robot!"

It took many hours to program this skillset
that you and I think of as run-of-the-mill – yet
through trial and error and lots of bruised fruit
this computerized process began to take root.

The outcome: a showcase of robotic frippery,
denuding a fruit often thought of as slippery.
But here's what we need, says the kitchen klatch chorus:
"A droid that cooks broccoli – and then eats it for us."

Just For Pun

No uniting theme to these final entries other than they all make extensive use of the alphabet.

Don't Ass, Don't Yell
(January 20, 2014)

Certainly you remember the now-abandoned "Don't Ask, Don't Tell" policy in our military, which was essentially a way for our government to stick its fingers in its ears and go "LA-LA-LA-LA-LA!" whenever the subject of a soldier's sexual orientation came up.

Would that I'd be so diffident when it comes to the subject of my recent colonoscopy — so get those fingers in place now.

I'm sure you're familiar with the concept of a colonoscopy, but have you actually had one? The CDC (part of the same government that came up with "LA-LA-LA-LA-LA!") recommends regular screenings for men and women, regardless of sexual orientation, starting at age 50. Why age 50? It's an implied half-way point of life, so does this mean the government thinks I'm going to live to be 100? That comes as a surprise to me. A recent article says half of all babies born today will live to be 100. The other half will live to have regular colonoscopies performed on them.

Everyone who's had a colonoscopy, or is familiar with the procedure, knows that "the prep" is the worst part of the process. You can't eat any solid foods the day before; clear liquids and JELL-O only. Then, that evening, you drink 4 liters of a "bowel cleansing" solution, and after a while you run repeatedly to the bathroom to, as your mother used to say, "make." (The solution comes in two flavors: pineapple and "regular." My pharmacy provided me with the "regular" — once reconstituted, I recognized the taste as Pine-Sol.) Over the course of several hours you'll make at least a dozen trips to the bathroom. The solution turns your gastrointestinal tract into a garden hose, with the spigot all the way open. I've already provided too much detail here and so will leave this section of our narrative with the words I shared with a friend: "I'm glad that shit's over."

The actual procedure is almost anti-climactic, since they give you the good drugs just before starting to poke around in your hoo-hah, and actual memories of this hideous violation are almost non-existent. I remember being a little nervous when the anesthesiologist told me he'd be using Propofol, the drug that became infamous due to its association with Michael Jackson's death, but ironically my anxiety was relieved by the administration of that very drug. During a prior colonoscopy I was given Versed which, as a layperson, I thought was pretty freakin' awesome. However, that drug will induce only "conscious sedation" versus the state of "deep sedation" Propofol provides. Conscious sedation is defined as when "the patient responds purposefully to verbal command," and deep sedation is when "the patient cannot be easily aroused, but responds purposefully following repeated or painful stimulation." As it relates to my procedure, under conscious sedation the gastroenterologist says, "John, please move your hips forward. John, can you move your hips forward?" and I dreamily move my hips forward. Under deep sedation, the gastroenterologist goes, "John (pokes with probe), move! (Pokes) Move! (POKES) MOVE, DAMMIT!"

By the way — it just struck me that the word "enter" is found in the middle of "gastroenterologist." That's kinda funny.

After the procedure ended (!), I was moved to a recovery room that I call the "Man Cave" since the nurse told me it was perfectly acceptable to fart as much as I felt necessary. I did so, and then some. As I awaited discharge (here by which I mean permission to leave the hospital), another patient was moved into the space next to me. I overheard some conversation between a nurse and doctor (HIPAA violation!) that the gentleman had been brought back for a second attempt at the procedure since, during his appointment the day before, he "wasn't clean." As there was also discussion about his need for a Vietnamese interpreter, I presumed they hadn't been referring to his sense of humor. I can only imagine what that experience must be like for the colon team… The patient's been sedated, buttocks aligned just so, the doctor slips the scope in and WHAT THE FU…?!?! Maybe due to the language barrier this guy thought he only needed to gargle with the prep solution.

Anyway, my results were good and I won't have to repeat the process for another five years. I'm referring to the colonoscopy — I intend to maintain my usual pace of farting. If you haven't already, this is where I'd recommend you stick your fingers in your ears, and maybe you should also step out of the room.

Blow Me
(February 4, 2014)

I recently had another birthday and again wasn't gifted with what I really wanted — an harmonica.

I've been hinting at wanting one for many years, having offered subtle hints and suggestions along the lines of:

- "Wow! Did you hear that guy wailing on an harmonica? Sure wish I had one so I could learn to play."
- "Honey, do you know anyone who plays an harmonica? No? Well, I know what would change that…"
- "What would I like for my birthday? Gee, I'd really love an harmonica."

Now, please don't think I'm one of those "make a fuss over me because it's My Special Day" sort of people — I'm not, I'm really not. Quite frankly, I'd be happiest if there were no acknowledgment whatsoever regarding the occasion. Birthdays are an odd celebration to begin with since the accomplishment they are recognizing is that you managed not to die during the previous year. It's an anniversary, but not like a wedding anniversary — a wedding anniversary is supposed to commemorate that one or the other of you managed to attract a mate and, despite your in-laws' efforts to the contrary, continue to live together and possibly even share a joint checking account. There's some effort involved. It's something you choose to do. The "event" that perhaps merits celebration regarding our births should be the anniversary of the date when our parents decided to engage in the act of sexual congress that later resulted in our slippery entrance into the world. For many of you, your parents were so enamored of each other that their passion resulted in you being born just nine months after they married. Or, in my case, being born just six months after.

A birthday is different – none of us choose to be born, much less on a specific date. A birthday just means you managed to plod through another 12 months of dreary existence on this earth while avoiding being sneezed upon and contracting swine flu, or run over by a bus, or "accidentally" mixing prescription drugs and cinnamon schnapps. What little effort may have been expended in these avoidance maneuvers is minimal at most. So, cheerful sort that I am, I'm happy for my birthday to be just another ordinary day of avoiding sneezes and buses. But — if my wife or son asks, "What do you want for your birthday?" and I offer a gentle and unobtrusive suggestion such as "I'd like some warm socks" or "I'd enjoy going out for a hamburger" or, most significantly, "I'D LIKE AN HARMONICA," then dammit! they'd better gimme those socks/that burger/AN HARMONICA.

Actual conversation, reproduced verbatim and occurs every year:

> WIFE: "What kind of birthday cake would you like?"
> ME: "I'd like a JELL-O cake."
> WIFE: "I am not making you a JELL-O cake."

She says a JELL-O cake is "gross." Well, I think potato salad is "gross" but I don't tell her she can't eat it, especially if she asked for it for her birthday (although I would not allow her to eat it anywhere within a thousand-yard proximity to me). Why doesn't she just tell me what kind of cake *she* would enjoy for my birthday? And then ask me to go to the store and pick it up?

See, this is exactly the kind of fracas I want to avoid by sidestepping the societal obligation to "celebrate" my birthday. It creates tension, angst, dissent, tumult… all feelings that leave me feeling rather blue. And what instrument best captures the essence of the blues? AN HARMONICA.

Am I the only one who sees the irony here? The one gift in the whole world that would make me happiest is precisely what I need to express my despair. Receiving an harmonica would fill me with such joy that I'd no longer have any need to play it.

Perhaps what I should get for my birthday is an oxymoron. Especially since I'm now starting to feel like one.

The Right to Bare Arms
(March 26, 2014)

I was shot in the workplace the other day by someone who didn't know how to properly use a gun. This really happened.

Granted, it was a Nerf gun shooting a foam-bodied projectile with a plastic tip — but it still hurt like hell. My "friend" (ha!) at work picked up the Nerf gun, which was lying on top of a small storage cabinet between my desk and my neighbor's, and started to play with it while waiting for me to finish an email before heading out together for a coffee break. I was focused on my desktop monitor and suddenly SMACK!!! the Nerf projectile struck me in the side of my neck. It had been "accidentally" (ha!) fired about 18 inches away from my head. My "friend" (ha!)

shrieked in dismay once the weapon discharged, and I let loose with a series of expletives that would surely land me a part in the next Martin Scorsese movie.

The perpetrator (new name for my "friend") apologized profusely and then offered the following excuses:

- "I was just playing around with it."
- "I didn't know it was loaded."
- "I didn't know how to operate it properly."
- "I never fired a Nerf gun before."
- "It shouldn't have been out in the open."
- "You were sitting too close to it when it went off."

OK, that last one I made up but the perp rattled off all the rest of them. The shooter attempted to absolve herself of any personal responsibility for the situation, so blaming the victim was sure to be next in her series of disingenuous statements if we hadn't already made it to the coffee shop by then. There was a quick reference to how she'd "Dick Cheney'd" me, alluding to the former Vice President's hunting accident some years back where he blasted a companion with a load of buckshot. If you recall, the victim in that shooting later apologized to Cheney, saying he was sorry "for all that Vice President Cheney and his family [had] to go through." Well, I'm not planning to apologize to my assailant, that's for sure.

Plus, the only thing my family had to endure were spasms of laughter when I told them I'd been shot with a Nerf.

Bitcoin, Broketooth
(December 17, 2017)

My son Josh, who is younger than I am, told me about something called "bitcoin" years ago. I didn't understand it then, and I don't understand it now — but if I'd displayed any confidence in what he told me back then, I'd be a very rich man today. Of course, it's understandable that I didn't take financial advice from someone who also used to try and get me to believe he routinely finished all his homework on the bus ride home. Especially since he walked to school.

Back when the boy first mentioned this virtual currency, it was virtually worthless — a value of less than one cent. But as of three seconds ago, one bitcoin was worth over $19,000 US dollars. That kind of exponential growth is the equivalent of going to get one of those Mylar balloons inflated for a party and walking out with something roughly the size of the moon. But then you'd have to figure out how to get it in your car, so there's that to consider.

I have a friend who lives in the Seattle area, who told me years ago many of his co-workers were investing in a startup called "Microsoft" — and at the time he thought it was a dubious prospect. Today his long-retired co-workers are all millionaires, but he comforts himself with the knowledge that there are no greater riches than the love shared among members of one's own family. Of course, no member of his family has spoken to him in the decades since he failed to turn them on to this stock tip.

You hear stories every now and then about someone who renovates a house and discovers a box stuffed with cash hidden behind the sheetrock, or finds out a painting purchased at a garage sale for five dollars is actually an Old Master and is worth millions. The only thing I ever found behind the sheetrock when renovating a house was mold and a huge bee colony. It cost me the small fortune I didn't find to get it all fixed.

But back to this bitcoin… I still don't understand how one acquires a bitcoin, or bitcoins, or a fractional amount of a bitcoin, or even how to balance my checkbook. Like most kids, I went through a coin-collecting phase, hoping to come across a wheat penny or a Franklin half-dollar. I actually had a few dozen silver dollars, some dating back to the mid-1800s, but cashed most of them in when I was a high school freshman and wanted to take an older girl out on a date. I strode into the bank, swinging my sack (of silver dollars; come on, now… As Sarah Sanders says, only someone with their mind in the gutter would think what you just thought), and asked the teller to exchange the collectible silver dollars for some spendable paper ones. She looked at me for a while and then asked, "Are you sure you want to do that?" I nodded in the affirmative, quite certain I was making the correct, lust-driven decision. I took the girl to the movies, purchased our tickets with a sure-to-impress-her crisp $20 bill, and somehow managed to throw the considerable amount of change I got back into the trash. We went to get our popcorn, candy, and sodas and when I went to flash my wad (tut-tut, people!), I had nothing but thirty-seven cents in change in my pocket. It may not come as a surprise to you that this lissome lass was never seen in my company again.

Anyway — needless to say, I am not a bitcoin billionaire today. I, like most not-to-the-manor-born folks, am struggling to understand how the seemingly inevitable passage of The Tax Cut and Jobs Act is going to impact my finances. I keep seeing (largely already wealthy) GOP folks on TV who keep claiming it'll be a boon to the middle class, saying, "Just plug in the numbers" to see how much of a tax break we'll get. Plug the numbers into what? A wall socket? Where's the prototype of the postcard-sized 1040 form that Paul Ryan keeps pulling out of his baggy suit jacket that I could use to quickly calculate my hypothetical tax relief?

I think this so-called "great Christmas gift" the Prez and GOP want to give us is as illusory as that postcard. And, just like with bitcoin — I'm not going to bite.

Smoke Scream
(March 30, 2018)

Our son Josh arrived for a visit during the last holiday season with a bag full of dirty laundry but nothing else resembling gifts. "Did you leave your other satchel on the train?" I asked him. He shook his head no, but informed us he had a very special present for us this time — he was giving up smoking.

This came as welcome news; my wife is a long-since reformed smoker, I have never smoked, and it's always been a concern of ours that he took up with cigarettes. "That's wonderful, son," I responded. "What prompted you to quit?" He told us he was doing so because he was broke and couldn't afford another pack.

It now seemed as though the core issue was less about smoking cessation and more about income cessation. But his finances are a topic for another day. Regardless of the motivation, we were pleased by his decision. "What's your strategy for quitting?" I inquired. "Medication? Hypnosis? Vaping, which so far as I know is exactly the same thing as smoking except for the smell?" He informed us he was going cold turkey. I told him I admired this challenging approach, encouraging him to let us know what we could do to help. He responded by asking if we could fix him a cold turkey sandwich. With some chips. And a bowl of tomato soup. And maybe grill the sandwich.

While responding to this request, I quickly calculated this food-based approach to weaning him from his addiction was going to cost me more than he ever spent on ciggies, so I suggested he instead try nicotine gum and offered to front his first week's supply. He accepted my offer, so after fixing him a follow-up ham and swiss on rye with a side of potato salad, I drove to the drugstore to make my purchase.

Now, as I mentioned up top — I've never smoked, so have no idea how much cigarettes cost. My only experience with purchasing them came when I was a youngster and would troop into the grocery store with my father, who would routinely buy two cartons of Kents every Christmas and birthday for my aunt Ruth, his older sister. He'd wrap the packages; she'd unwrap them and always feign surprise at the gift. Back then, a carton of smokes cost around three dollars (adjusted for inflation, roughly the equivalent of $15-$16 today). Josh told me he pays over ten dollars a pack after the sales and other taxes assessed in Boston, where he lives, are applied. He's not a heavy smoker, copping only to a pack or so a week. He seems to burn through them at a higher rate when he comes for a visit, but perhaps that's his way of dealing with the stress from his parents' constant admonitions regarding his nasty habit.

Anyway — I share the math above because, as I learned at the drug store, the nicotine gum is not a cheaper alternative. The cost of one piece of gum and one cigarette, depending on the brand of each, is roughly the same. No doubt the manufacturers had a very easy time coming up with the price of their product: "We have an addicted population that is already spending an inordinate amount for multiple fixes every day, so why should we sell our 'cure' for any less?" God bless our capitalist system.

My wife has a relative who quit smoking after (this may not come as a shock) developing lung cancer. He's survived two bouts of the disease (and, to his credit, did not take up smoking again in-between occurrences), and has made other lifestyle choices to aid in his long-term recovery. He shocked us during a recent visit by telling us he used to smoke four packs A DAY; he'd finish one and immediately light the next, from the moment he got up in the morning until he went to bed at night. The only time I was ever that busy with my hands was shortly after the onset of puberty, when… umm, let's just say — I stumbled upon an alternate and almost-as-addictive method of stimulating my brain's pleasure centers.

I brought home the gum and Josh began chewing tablets between sandwiches. Before leaving to go home, he said he was feeling better without smoking and had even begun to taper down on the number of pieces he required each day to deal with his cravings. His mom and I were very pleased with this news and offered him our well-wishes for a complete and successful withdrawal.

Fast-forward two months from that visit, when Josh called us one day to say a quick hello during a break at work. As we chatted about what was new in our respective households, we overheard a muffled voice entering the conversation. "Who was that?" my wife asked. "Oh, just someone bumming a cigarette from me," he replied. We were disheartened to realize the attempt to quit hadn't taken, but kept our opinion to ourselves this time. Our son is an adult, responsible for his own choices, with the apron strings severed long ago.

But I'll be damned if I'm going to let that turkey eat his way through three pounds of cold cuts the next time he visits for a weekend. Chew on that, sonny boy.

Speaker of the Hows
(August 11, 2018)

I know several people who, among their various talents, list availability as a "motivational speaker." That sounds like a pretty sweet gig and I'm thinking of hanging out my metaphorical shingle. Of course, the first thing I need to decide is: how much can I pull in for one of these talks?

The second consideration would, of necessity, be the content of the message I intend to convey. What is it I feel qualified to motivate others to accomplish? What gripping personal story will I share (or borrow from an old copy of *Reader's Digest*) and relate to a universal "life lesson"? How can I establish an intimate connection with an audience numbering in the hundreds, nay thousands, when I really don't care for most people on an individual basis?

I believe, in all modesty, and not using this post as an example, that I am most qualified to motivate ~~suckers~~ people to use humor and positive thinking as a way to cope in moments of despair:

- I was laid off from my job. Great! Now you have time to write that novel!
- I think my spouse is being unfaithful. Great! Now you don't need to bother with "date night" anymore!
- My business went into bankruptcy. Great! Now you are qualified to run for President of the United States!
- I've just been diagnosed with a fatal illness. Great! Now you can… uh, well, actually — that sorta sucks.

I'm just spit-balling here; I may need to refine my approach a skosh.

There are several well-known quotes regarding motivation, which I'm sure you can find on the internet since I don't feel like taking the time to search for them at the moment.

The best part of billing yourself as a motivational speaker: you have zero accountability for any observable improvement in the lives of those who attend your talks. Fly in, spend the night in a nice hotel, take to the stage amidst wild applause, captivate the crowd, bask in a standing ovation once you're done, and fly out. An hour later, folks may have only a vague recollection of what they just heard — but _you_ will be settling into the plush business class seat specified in your contract while staring googly-eyed at the long string of zeros punctuated by commas on the cashier's check you pocketed upon your departure. Easy peasy.

Years ago, my wife and I went to hear Dr. Leo Buscaglia speak in Schenectady, New York (motto: "We're not certain how to spell it, either") at Proctors Theatre. This was early in our marriage, back when we couldn't keep our hands off each other, which made the drive there challenging. At that time, Buscaglia was a ubiquitous presence on public television, sharing his message regarding the importance of showing love to yourself and those around you. Among his nicknames, he was known as the "Hug Doctor" due to his propensity for offering a warm embrace to every member of the audience who turned out to hear him. The moment he concluded the talk we attended, a woman seated in the third row rushed toward the stage like a defensive lineman: hurdling over seats, elbowing others out of her way, and knocking people over so she could be the first recipient of his post-lecture affections. Her actions seemed somewhat at odds with the message Dr. Buscaglia had just conveyed. I'm open to making brief eye contact with my future acolytes, but times are different now and another provision in my contract will be for a metal detector positioned stage right.

I don't have an advanced degree, so I suppose I'll have to put quotation marks around the honorific listed on my promotional materials:

- "Dr." John Branning / Bored-Certified
- John Branning, "Esq." / Little Gator
- "Rev." John Branning / God-Awful

Anyway, I'll wrap this up since I'm feeling motivated to get started on my presentation and fee schedule. If you're interested in booking me for what will be an inspirational yet surprisingly brief appearance, let me know and I'll send a link to my PayPal account to secure your non-refundable deposit. Sorry, the "Meet & Greet" is only for those who paid extra for a VIP pass.

Holland Tunnel Vision
(May 17, 2019)

Researchers at Ohio State University… excuse me—THE Ohio State University, determined via a recent study of Nobel Prize laureates in economics that there are two different life cycles of creativity, one that hits some people in their mid-20s and another that peaks in their mid-50s.

I have a few questions:

- Creativity in economics? I thought "creative accounting" was grounds for a tax audit.
- Aren't "laureates" what cowboys use to rope cattle?
- The early and later peaks cited here are thirty years apart. What happens during this extended fallow period? Economists struggle to balance their checkbooks like the rest of us?

The researchers also make a distinction between "conceptual" and "experimental" innovators. Conceptual innovators think outside the box, and experimental innovators climb inside the box to play with the packing peanuts. Conceptual innovators tend to peak creatively in their younger years, with experimental innovators doing so later in life.

I have a few more questions:

- What is the difference between "ovation" and "innovation"? Is innovation when you give your B&B a 5-star review on TripAdvisor?
- How could a technical article on the science of creativity include the cliché "think outside the box"?
- Will the Right-To-Life folks now proclaim that innovation begins at the moment of conception?

The complete study appears in a journal published in the Netherlands called *De Economist* (which, translated from the Dutch, means *Sleepy Time*). Another recent article from the same publication is entitled, "A Note on Artificial Pitches and Home Advantage in Dutch Professional Football," so perhaps I was mistaken and, in Holland, the word *economist* means *bookie*.

The last of my questions:

- Why are the Netherlands also known as Holland? And isn't it interesting that, if I reverse the question ("Why is Holland also known as the Netherlands?"), "Holland" takes the singular present tense of the verb "to be" versus the plural form required by "the Netherlands"?
- And how does the use of "Dutch" fit into all this? In response to the question, "Does it bother you that your country is known as both 'Holland' and 'the Netherlands'?" would the answer be, "No, not that Dutch."
- Does the song "Pass the Dutchie on the Left Hand Side" refer to where vehicles should be positioned while driving in the Holland? Sorry… I mean in Netherlands?
- Isn't Netherlands where Peter Pan lived? Sorry… I mean Ronald "Dutch" Reagan?

I guess it's becoming clear here that I'm nowhere near anything resembling a creative peak, and let's leave my age out of it.

Whatever You Do, Don't Faucet
(August 14, 2019)

Recently, the kitchen sink faucet started to drip… drip… drip. While I found the gentle, rhythmic sound of water splashing on stainless steel quite comforting, Carol found it markedly less so and ~~commanded~~ politely requested I fix it.

Now, I am willing to admit I'm not the handiest of guys around the house – and there are several plastered-over holes in the walls and a wobbly fan dangling from the living room ceiling attesting to that. But a leaky faucet is the first item listed in the syllabus for Home Repair 101, so I dusted the cobwebs off of my toolbox and got to work.

I know what you're thinking: "I bet he forgot to turn off the water before removing the faucet handles!" Really – you think that little of me? No need to answer; it's a rhetorical question.

Once I had everything disassembled and didn't see any obvious points of failure, I considered Occam's razor and figured I would just clean the small bits of crud off the assorted parts before putting them back together, believing that was the most parsimonious solution. I soaked, scrubbed, and rinsed each component, reassembled the structure, turned the water valves back on (which I *had* remembered to turn off, O ye of little faith!) – and immediately saw a thin but now-steady flow of water emanating from the faucet, despite both handles being in the "off" position. I'd managed to turn a minor inconvenience into a major problem; that's my specialty.

I took it all apart again, made sure everything was snugly in place and re-assembled, turned the water supply on, spun the taps – and had now restored the original threat level of an occasional drip. While tempted to declare this a Trump-like victory, I decided to give it one more shot and so took everything apart for the third time. I believe this action qualified me as a "master" plumber since I now had the process down cold.

However, this time before reassembling I paused briefly to see if there were any online references suggesting an alternate course of action. I found a repair video for a sink that looked identical to mine, posted by another home handyman. The video displayed slick production values, as text scrolled across the screen which read, "PLEASE IGNORE HOW DIRTY MY SINK IS!" His kitchen counters looked as if they had last been scrubbed during the Bush (41) administration. Nevertheless, he chose to post this video – warts, scum and all – but actually provided the useful piece of information that the seat and spring beneath the cartridge were the likely source of the problem and should be replaced.

All well and good, but since I was home without a car I couldn't zip to the hardware store for replacements. Therefore, I put everything back in place so we could use the sink until I had a chance to pick up the parts, turning on the sink one last time to ensure I hadn't made the problem worse again.

The outcome here depends upon your definition of "problem" – apparently, I'd reversed the cartridges this go-round, and so both handles now spun the opposite way when starting the flow of hot and cold water. "Dang it all!" is not the phrase I shouted in response to this kerfuffle. Well, since the drip was no worse, and I was going to have to take the sink apart to install the new parts anyway, I figured I'd just leave things in this alternate-universe state until then. But the error gnawed at me… and, quite frankly, I did not want to face my wife's understandable scorn when she came from work to find that I didn't even know how to put everything back together correctly while still having only a hunch regarding a fix for the core issue.

And so – I took the faucet apart for the fourth time, correctly oriented the cartridges, and put all back in place. By this time, the jaws of my plumber's wrench were practically glowing red from repeated use. I turned the handles one last time to ensure they moved in the correct direction, which (and this may surprise you) they did. But when I turned off the water flow there was one more shock still in store – the faucet was no longer leaking. Disbelieving my good fortune, I must've turned the water on and off a dozen times; the issue did not return. It's been 24 hours and still no evidence of the drip.

Flush with new-found confidence in my handyman skills, my plan for today is to open up our computer and see if I can figure out why the fan that cools the hard drive makes so much noise. I know what you're thinking, but you're wrong: I already backed up our files. I just need to remember where I stashed the floppy disks.

Macramé-be Not
(April 21, 2020)

In an attempt to put a bright, shiny face on this pandemic – I've been posting a series of DIY instructional videos illustrating how to master some artisanal crafts and household tasks that are seemingly beyond the ken for most of you.

The following "behind-the-scenes" commentaries may enhance your enjoyment of each tutorial:

How to Bake Bread
The recipe called for whole wheat flour; I mistakenly thought we had a bag in the pantry and so had to quickly identify a substitute since the yeast had already begun to proof. Solution: 1½ pounds of kibble run through the food processor on the "Pulse" setting yields four dry cups – resulting in a loaf with a moist crumb and glossy coat.

How to Change the Oil in Your Car
Make sure you are watching the updated version of this video, where I remember to replace the drain plug before adding five quarts of 10W30.

How to Cut Your Own Hair
In hindsight, I should have asked my wife to film this so I could have operated the clippers with my dominant hand. You'll be happy to know since posting this one that the bald spots and my left eyebrow have almost completely grown back.

How to Make Your Own Candles
I know this is a popular activity among crafters, but I found it rather pointless: all I did was light one candle, collect the drippings in an empty toilet paper roll, and then peel it away in order to create a second, stockier candle.

How to Fix a Leaky Sink
I don't think I stressed this strongly enough: turn off the hot and cold water feeds before beginning this process. As a result, you

may be interested in another of my videos: "*How to Repair a Water-Damaged Ceiling.*"

How to Grow Your Own Salad in a Raised Bed Garden
This one actually never came to fruition since my wife insisted I remove the soil, manure and chicken wire piled atop our mattress.

How to Build a Bookshelf
Since I don't consider myself an accomplished woodworker, I was really pleased with how this project turned out. The corners are square, the shelf is stable, and the deep walnut stain makes this a beautiful addition to our other home furnishings. My only regret after completion was wishing I'd thought to make it large enough to hold a second book.

How to Rewire a Table Lamp
While it took a few days, the neighborhood eventually had power restored.

How to Install a Garbage Disposal
As I explained in the video: count to make sure all the forks are back in the drawer before turning on the disposal for the first time.

How to Safely Use a Chainsaw
Under its Terms of Service, my internet provider removed this video for having content it deemed "graphic and/or disturbing." I'm in the final stages of editing its replacement: "*How to Get Reimbursed for an Out-Of-Network Emergency Room Visit.*"

Afterward

I ~~perversely~~ fervently hope you've enjoyed this book. At this moment, I'm reminded of something Socrates once said to me: "The comic and the tragic lie inseparably close, like light and shadow." So, if you found reading this to be a tragic experience, I take comfort in knowing I came *thisclose* to amusing you. Likewise, I imagine Socrates giggled all the way through chugging down that cup of hemlock.

There are days when I find everything funny; days when I find nothing funny at all – and then there are the days when my wife finds everything I do and say funny, but not in a good way.

Most of the laughs herein have been at my expense – by which I mean I paid out of pocket to have this book published. There were also a few at Trump's expense, but he – allegedly – can afford them (although he appears to be bereft of any sense of humor, particularly about himself). I have come to recognize that many of my observations that I initially considered clever and/or insightful were actually obnoxious and/or juvenile. But, as they say ("they," in this case, being neither Socrates nor Trump), the first step in solving a problem is to admit that you have one. I am willing to do so right here and right now: I cop to having <u>one</u> problem. There, I feel much better now.

I offer thanks to my family, friends, former co-workers, and other f-words for their boundless inspiration and much-less-frequent support.

Finally, I again harken back to Socrates and what he famously said about the unexamined life: "ο δέ ανεξέταστος βίος ου βιωτός ανθρώπω." I'm not sure what he meant, since it's all Greek to me.

JB

About the Author

John Branning is the author of five (well, now six) books of humor.

He attended three different elementary schools – not because of disciplinary infractions or because he belonged to a military family – but just because his parents were serial "movers" and often relocated during the week of spring break, leaving John to anxiously attempt to make new friends during the final weeks of the school year.

He spent many lonely summers as a youngster but doesn't bear any goddam resentment as a result.

An underachieving high schooler, an indifferent college student, and a resentful employee – fortunately, he met his wife Carol, who got him straightened out. For the most part.

The birth of his son Josh brought him much joy, eclipsed only by the adoption of seven cats who have lived with the family at various times over the years. As of the publication of this book, the cat population has dwindled to a mere two. John and Carol did not pick up any other stray children along the way.

John, Carol, Nate (cat), Josh (son), and Miles (other cat) currently live on a lake in central Maine, where they are all quite happy and occasionally ecstatic.

www.ingramcontent.com/pod-product-compliance
Lightning Source LLC
Chambersburg PA
CBHW020422010526
44118CB00010B/367